THE COMIC COLLECTION

A GERRY ANDERSON PRODUCTION

THUNDERBIRDS™

VOLUME ONE

EGMONT

CONTENTS

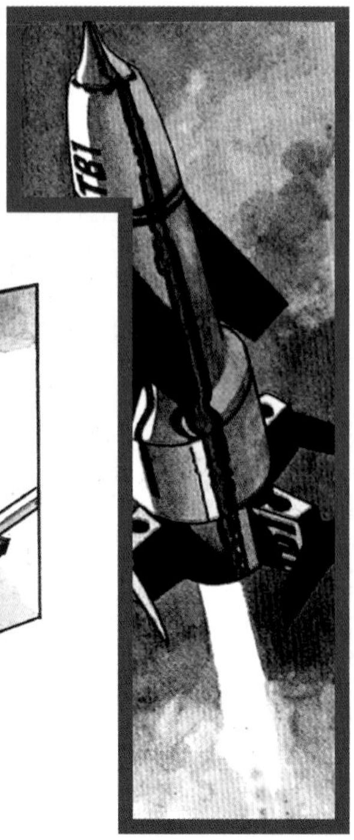

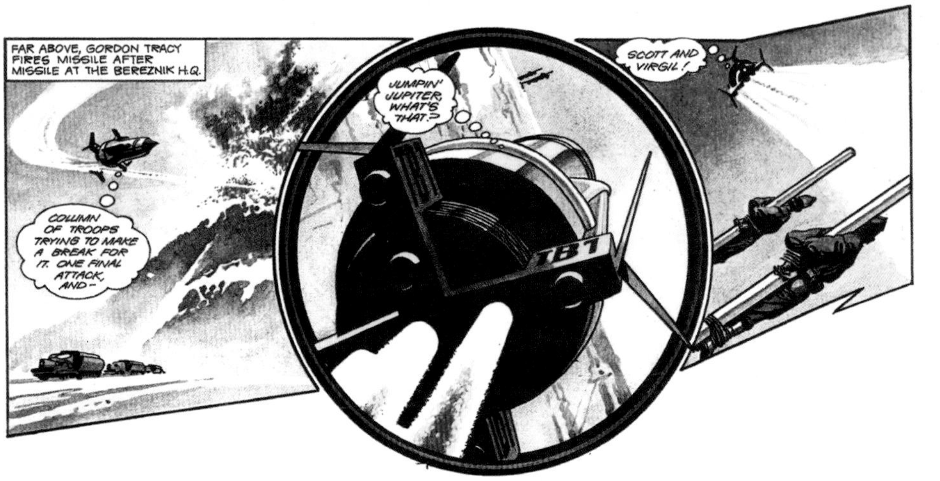

FAR ABOVE, GORDON TRACY FIRES MISSILE AFTER MISSILE AT THE BEREZNIK H.Q.
COLUMN OF TROOPS TRYING TO MAKE A BREAK FOR IT. ONE FINAL ATTACK, AND--
JUMPIN' JUPITER, WHAT'S THAT?
SCOTT AND VIRGIL!

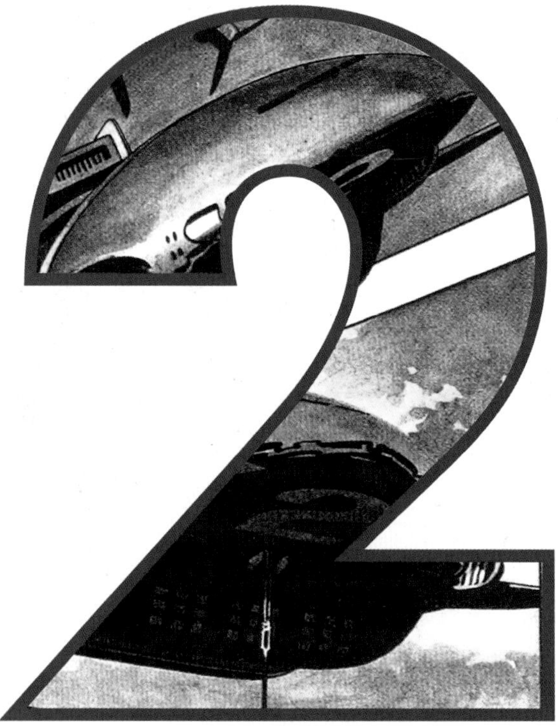

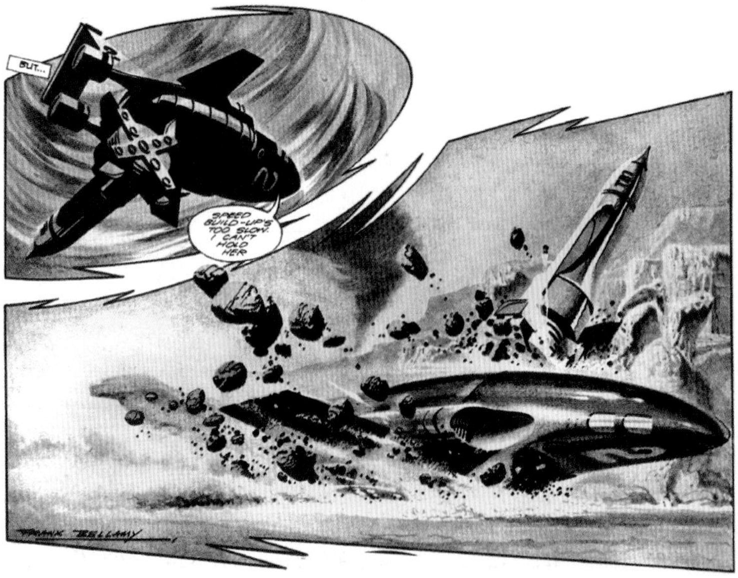

BUT...
SPEED BUILD-UP'S TOO SLOW. I CAN'T HOLD HER

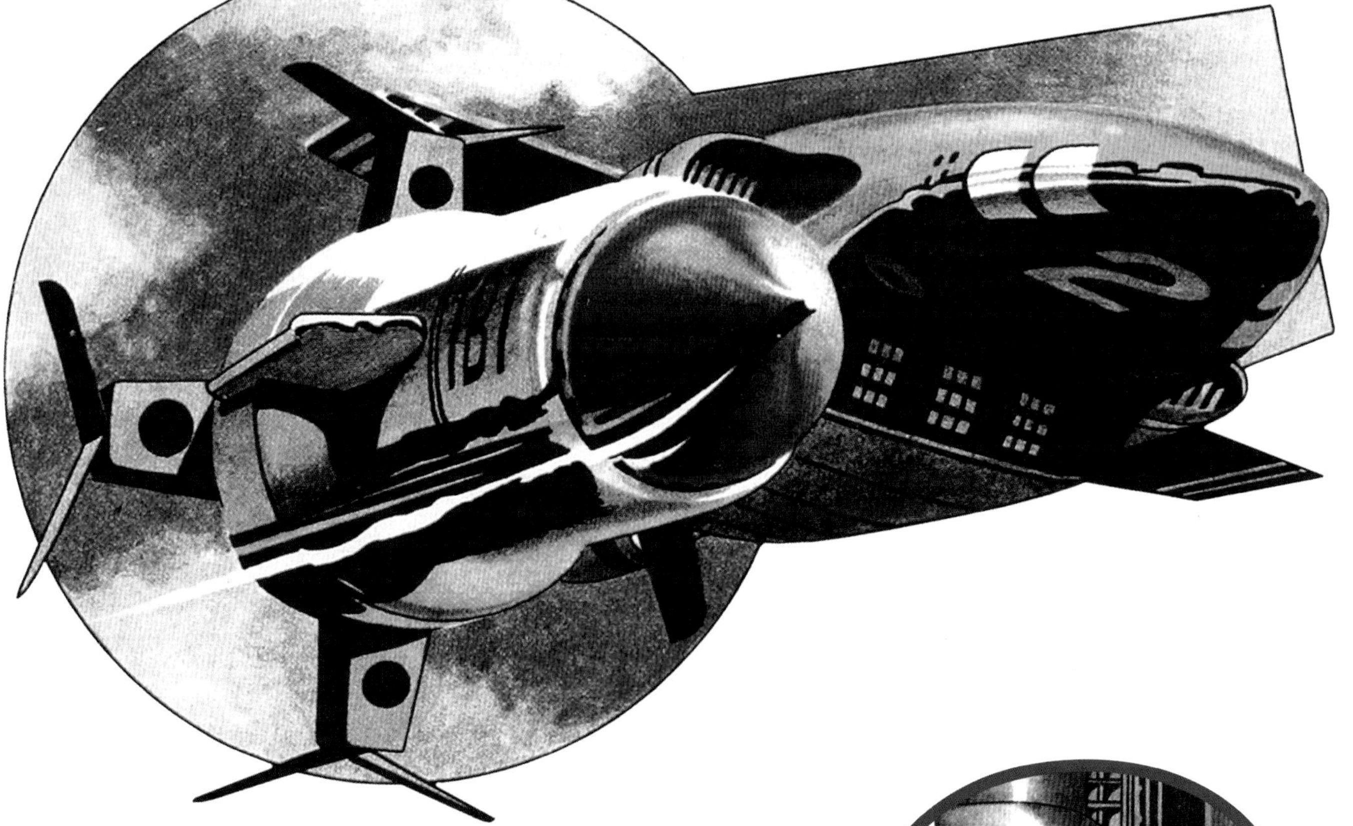

3

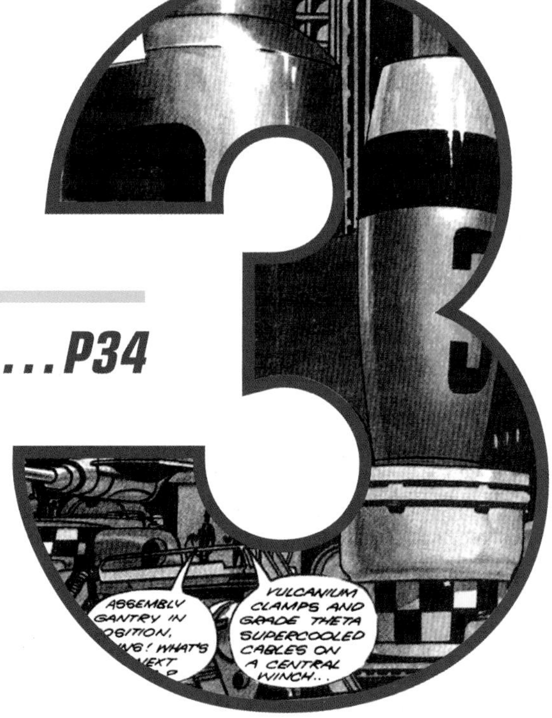
ASSEMBLY GANTRY IN
WHAT'S
VULCANIUM CLAMPS AND GRADE THETA SUPERCOOLED CABLES ON A CENTRAL WINCH...

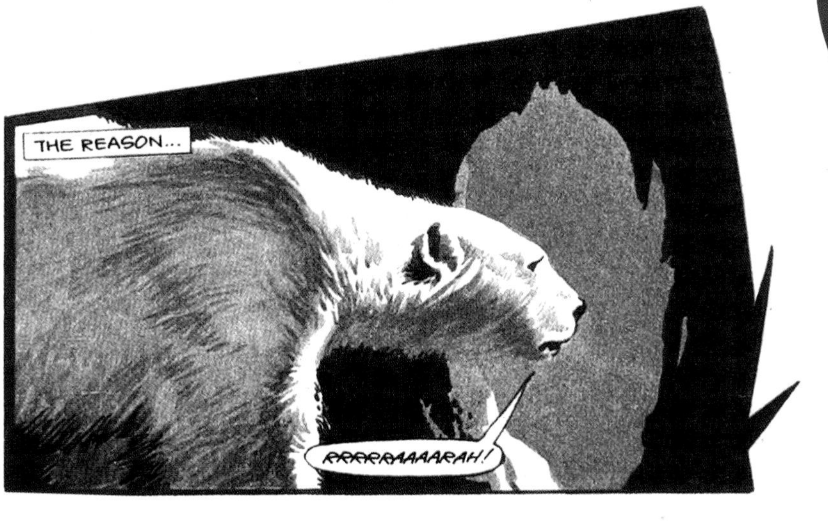
THE REASON...
RRRRRAAAAARAH!

Part 1 - dateline 30 September 2067

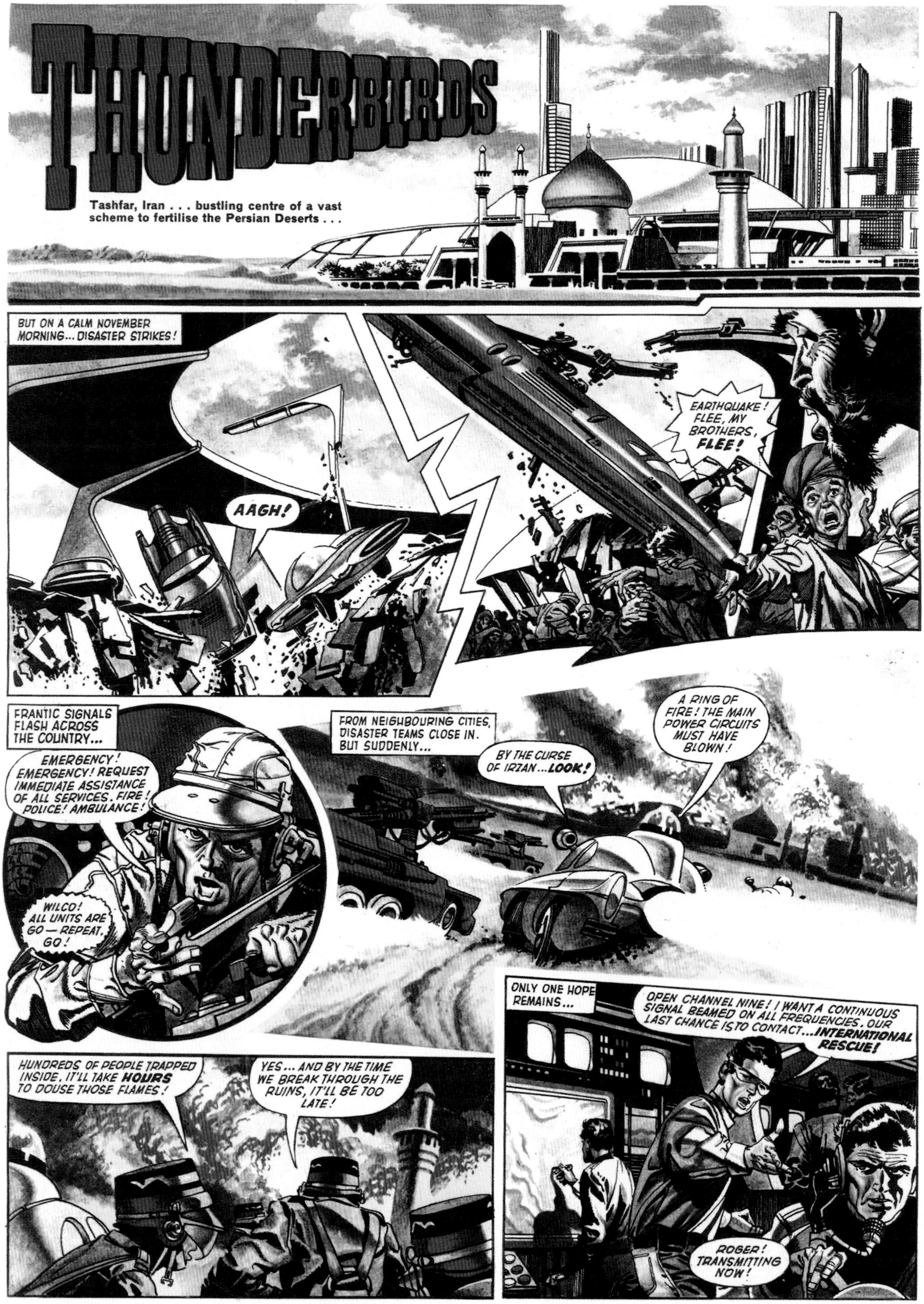
THUNDERBIRDS
Tashfar, Iran . . . bustling centre of a vast scheme to fertilise the Persian Deserts . . .
BUT ON A CALM NOVEMBER MORNING... DISASTER STRIKES!
AAGH!
EARTHQUAKE! FLEE, MY BROTHERS, FLEE!
FRANTIC SIGNALS FLASH ACROSS THE COUNTRY...
EMERGENCY! EMERGENCY! REQUEST IMMEDIATE ASSISTANCE OF ALL SERVICES. FIRE! POLICE! AMBULANCE!
WILCO! ALL UNITS ARE GO — REPEAT, GO!
FROM NEIGHBOURING CITIES, DISASTER TEAMS CLOSE IN. BUT SUDDENLY...
BY THE CURSE OF IRZAN...LOOK!
A RING OF FIRE! THE MAIN POWER CIRCUITS MUST HAVE BLOWN!
HUNDREDS OF PEOPLE TRAPPED INSIDE. IT'LL TAKE HOURS TO DOUSE THOSE FLAMES!
YES... AND BY THE TIME WE BREAK THROUGH THE RUINS, IT'LL BE TOO LATE!
ONLY ONE HOPE REMAINS...
OPEN CHANNEL NINE! I WANT A CONTINUOUS SIGNAL BEAMED ON ALL FREQUENCIES. OUR LAST CHANCE IS TO CONTACT... INTERNATIONAL RESCUE!
ROGER! TRANSMITTING NOW!

Artist: Frank Bellamy

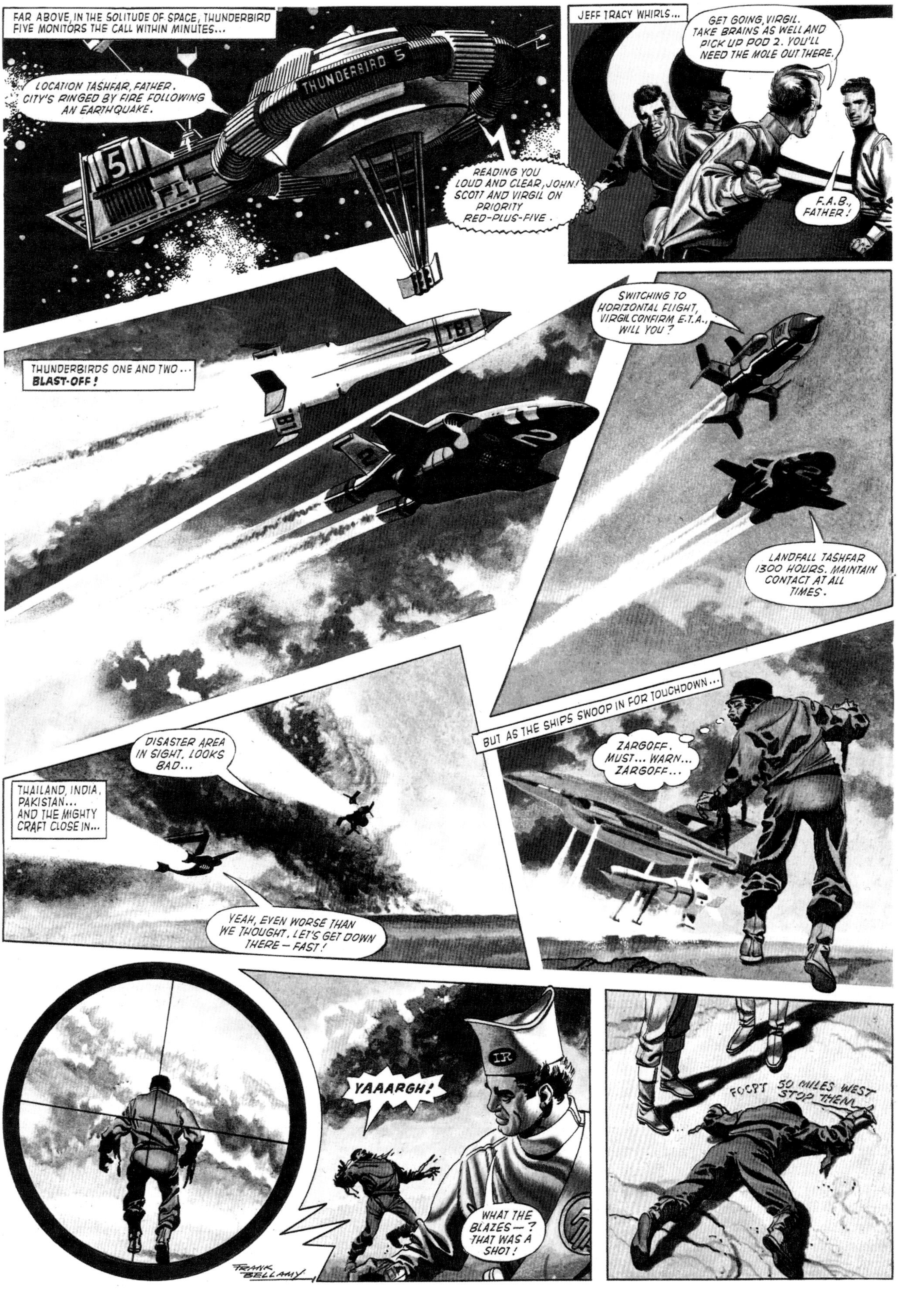
FAR ABOVE, IN THE SOLITUDE OF SPACE, THUNDERBIRD FIVE MONITORS THE CALL WITHIN MINUTES...
THUNDERBIRD 5
LOCATION TASHFAR, FATHER. CITY'S RINGED BY FIRE FOLLOWING AN EARTHQUAKE.
READING YOU LOUD AND CLEAR, JOHN! SCOTT AND VIRGIL ON PRIORITY RED-PLUS-FIVE.
JEFF TRACY WHIRLS...
GET GOING, VIRGIL. TAKE BRAINS AS WELL AND PICK UP POD 2. YOU'LL NEED THE MOLE OUT THERE.
F.A.B., FATHER!
THUNDERBIRDS ONE AND TWO ... **BLAST-OFF!**
SWITCHING TO HORIZONTAL FLIGHT, VIRGIL. CONFIRM E.T.A., WILL YOU?
LANDFALL TASHFAR 1300 HOURS. MAINTAIN CONTACT AT ALL TIMES.
THAILAND, INDIA, PAKISTAN... AND THE MIGHTY CRAFT CLOSE IN...
DISASTER AREA IN SIGHT. LOOKS BAD...
YEAH, EVEN WORSE THAN WE THOUGHT. LET'S GET DOWN THERE — FAST!
BUT AS THE SHIPS SWOOP IN FOR TOUCHDOWN...
ZARGOFF. MUST... WARN... ZARGOFF...
YAAARGH!
WHAT THE BLAZES —? THAT WAS A SHOT!
FRANK BELLAMY
FOCPT 50 MILES WEST STOP THEM

Part 2 - dateline 07 October 2067

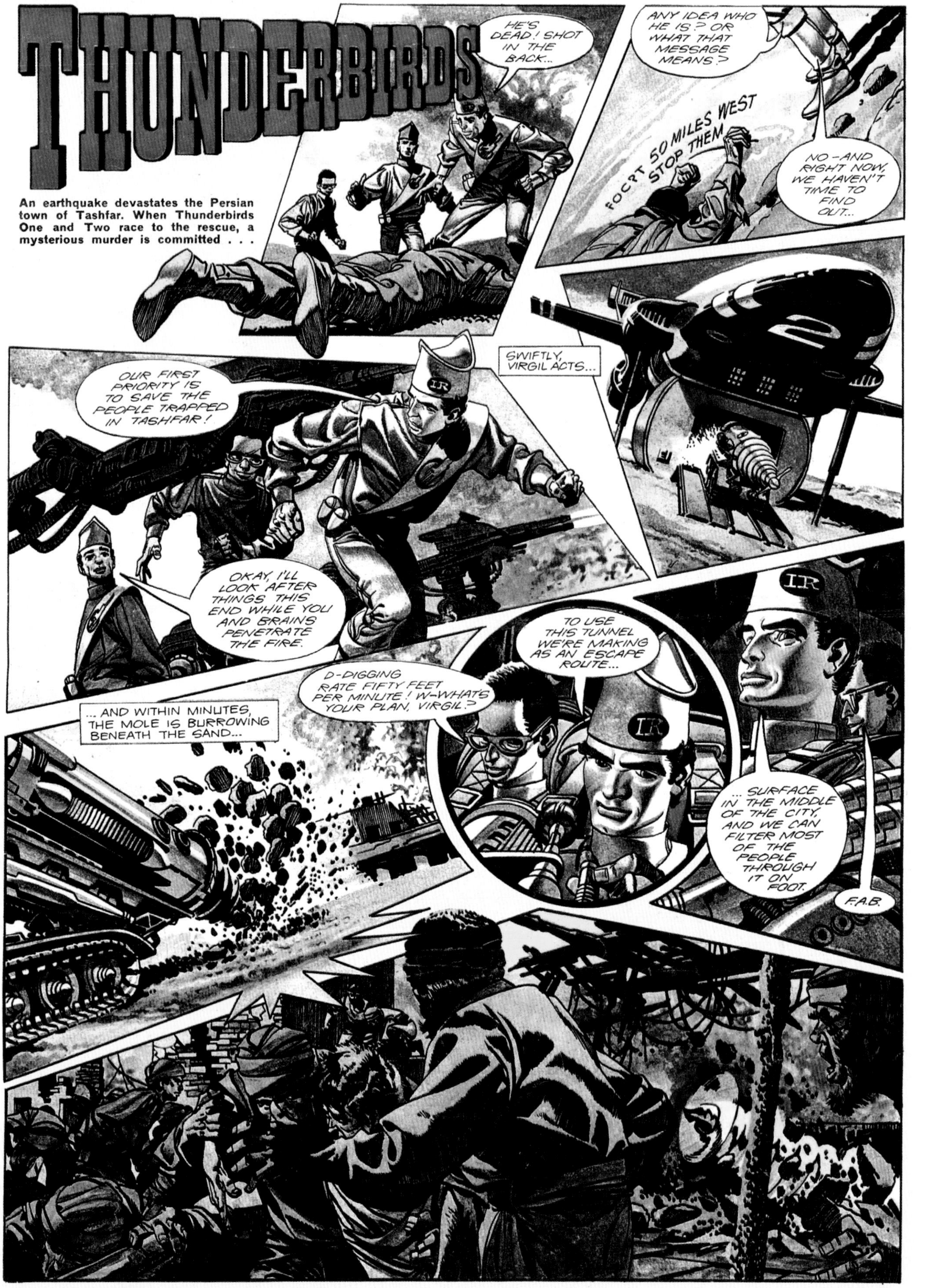
THUNDERBIRDS
An earthquake devastates the Persian town of Tashfar. When Thunderbirds One and Two race to the rescue, a mysterious murder is committed . . .
HE'S DEAD! SHOT IN THE BACK...
ANY IDEA WHO HE IS? OR WHAT THAT MESSAGE MEANS?
FOCPT 50 MILES WEST
STOP THEM
NO - AND RIGHT NOW, WE HAVEN'T TIME TO FIND OUT...
OUR FIRST PRIORITY IS TO SAVE THE PEOPLE TRAPPED IN TASHFAR!
OKAY, I'LL LOOK AFTER THINGS THIS END WHILE YOU AND BRAINS PENETRATE THE FIRE.
SWIFTLY, VIRGIL ACTS...
... AND WITHIN MINUTES, THE MOLE IS BURROWING BENEATH THE SAND...
D-DIGGING RATE FIFTY FEET PER MINUTE! W-WHAT'S YOUR PLAN, VIRGIL?
TO USE THIS TUNNEL WE'RE MAKING AS AN ESCAPE ROUTE...
... SURFACE IN THE MIDDLE OF THE CITY, AND WE CAN FILTER MOST OF THE PEOPLE THROUGH IT ON FOOT.
F.A.B.

Artist: Frank Bellamy

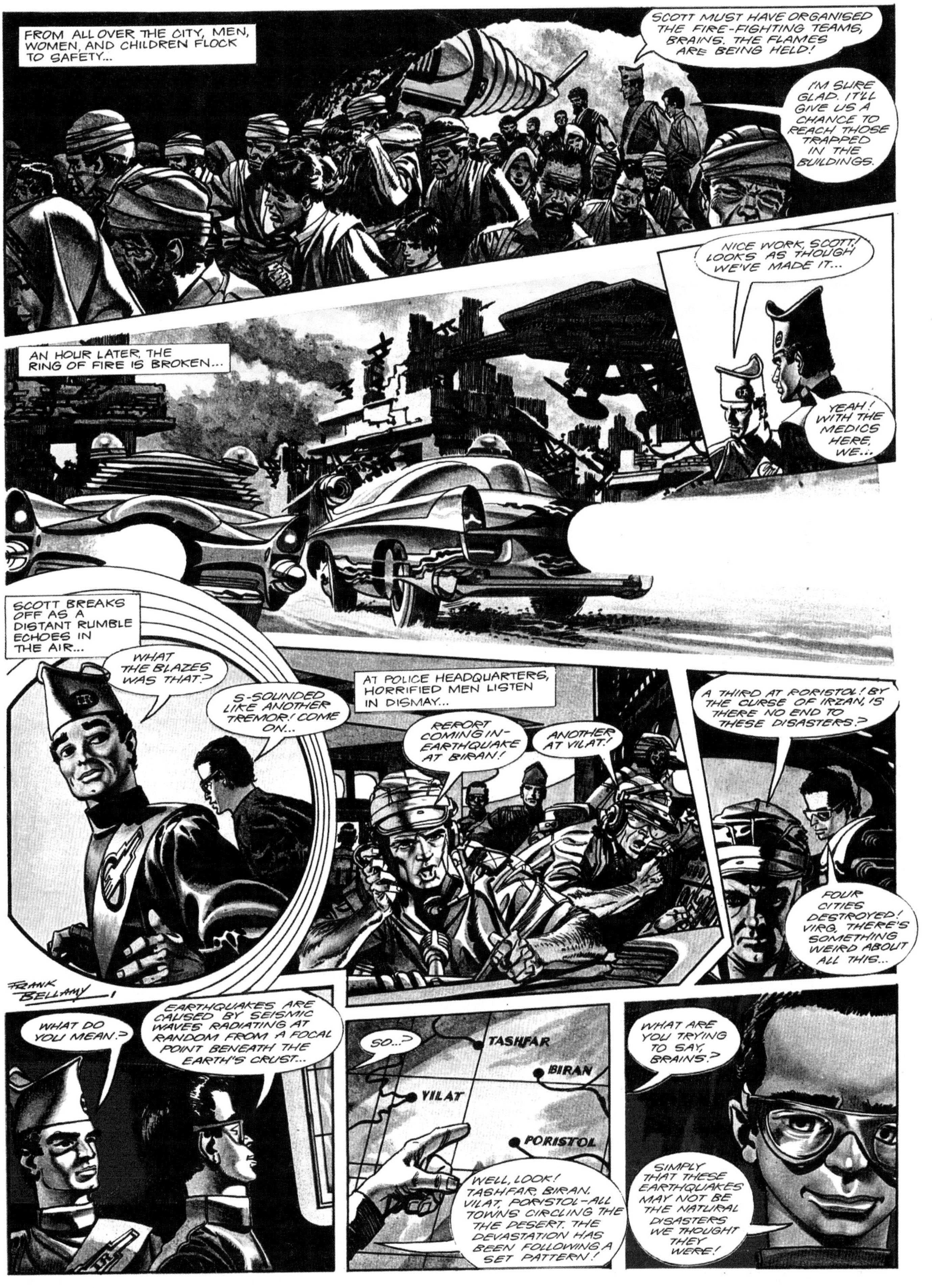
FROM ALL OVER THE CITY, MEN, WOMEN, AND CHILDREN FLOCK TO SAFETY...
SCOTT MUST HAVE ORGANISED THE FIRE-FIGHTING TEAMS, BRAINS. THE FLAMES ARE BEING HELD!
I'M SURE GLAD. IT'LL GIVE US A CHANCE TO REACH THOSE TRAPPED IN THE BUILDINGS.
AN HOUR LATER, THE RING OF FIRE IS BROKEN...
NICE WORK, SCOTT! LOOKS AS THOUGH WE'VE MADE IT...
YEAH! WITH THE MEDICS HERE, WE...
SCOTT BREAKS OFF AS A DISTANT RUMBLE ECHOES IN THE AIR...
WHAT THE BLAZES WAS THAT?
S-SOUNDED LIKE ANOTHER TREMOR! COME ON...
AT POLICE HEADQUARTERS, HORRIFIED MEN LISTEN IN DISMAY...
REPORT COMING IN- EARTHQUAKE AT BIRAN!
ANOTHER AT VILAT!
A THIRD AT PORISTOL! BY THE CURSE OF IRZAN, IS THERE NO END TO THESE DISASTERS?
FOUR CITIES DESTROYED! VIRG, THERE'S SOMETHING WEIRD ABOUT ALL THIS...
FRANK BELLAMY
WHAT DO YOU MEAN?
EARTHQUAKES ARE CAUSED BY SEISMIC WAVES RADIATING AT RANDOM FROM A FOCAL POINT BENEATH THE EARTH'S CRUST...
SO...?
TASHFAR
BIRAN
VILAT
PORISTOL
WELL, LOOK! TASHFAR, BIRAN, VILAT, PORISTOL-ALL TOWNS CIRCLING THE THE DESERT. THE DEVASTATION HAS BEEN FOLLOWING A SET PATTERN!
WHAT ARE YOU TRYING TO SAY, BRAINS?
SIMPLY THAT THESE EARTHQUAKES MAY NOT BE THE NATURAL DISASTERS WE THOUGHT THEY WERE!

Part 3 - dateline 14 October 2067

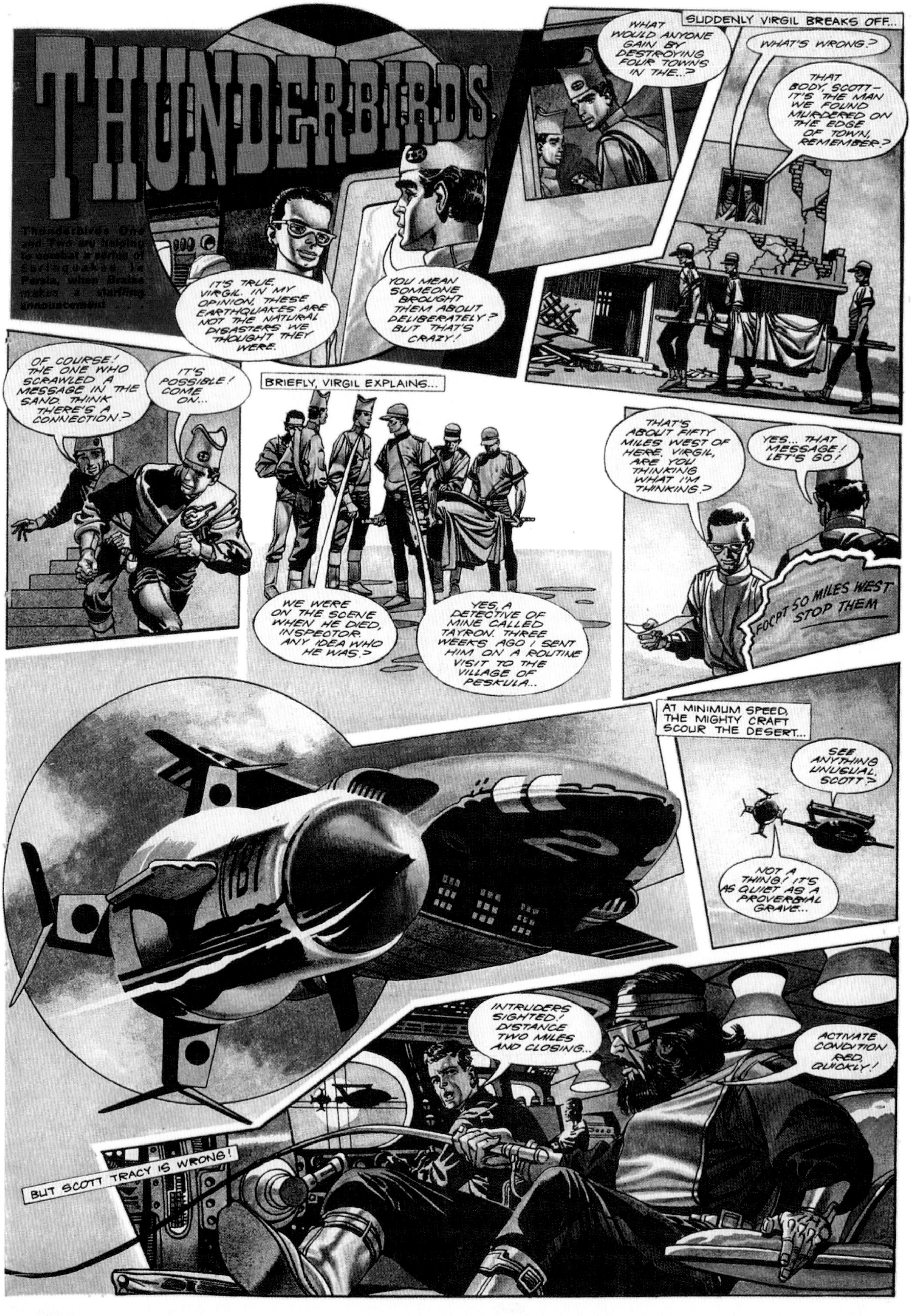
THUNDERBIRDS
Thunderbirds One and Two are helping to combat a series of earthquakes in Parsia, when Brains makes a startling announcement . . .
IT'S TRUE, VIRGIL. IN MY OPINION, THESE EARTHQUAKES ARE NOT THE NATURAL DISASTERS WE THOUGHT THEY WERE.
YOU MEAN SOMEONE BROUGHT THEM ABOUT DELIBERATELY? BUT THAT'S CRAZY!
WHAT WOULD ANYONE GAIN BY DESTROYING FOUR TOWNS IN THE...?
SUDDENLY VIRGIL BREAKS OFF...
WHAT'S WRONG?
THAT BODY, SCOTT— IT'S THE MAN WE FOUND MURDERED ON THE EDGE OF TOWN, REMEMBER?
OF COURSE! THE ONE WHO SCRAWLED A MESSAGE IN THE SAND. THINK THERE'S A CONNECTION?
IT'S POSSIBLE! COME ON...
BRIEFLY, VIRGIL EXPLAINS...
WE WERE ON THE SCENE WHEN HE DIED, INSPECTOR. ANY IDEA WHO HE WAS?
YES, A DETECTIVE OF MINE CALLED TAYRON. THREE WEEKS AGO I SENT HIM ON A ROUTINE VISIT TO THE VILLAGE OF PESKULA...
THAT'S ABOUT FIFTY MILES WEST OF HERE. VIRGIL, ARE YOU THINKING WHAT I'M THINKING?
YES... THAT MESSAGE! LET'S GO!
FOCPT 50 MILES WEST STOP THEM
AT MINIMUM SPEED, THE MIGHTY CRAFT SCOUR THE DESERT...
SEE ANYTHING UNUSUAL, SCOTT?
NOT A THING! IT'S AS QUIET AS A PROVERBIAL GRAVE...
BUT SCOTT TRACY IS WRONG!
INTRUDERS SIGHTED! DISTANCE TWO MILES AND CLOSING...
ACTIVATE CONDITION RED, QUICKLY!

Artist: Frank Bellamy

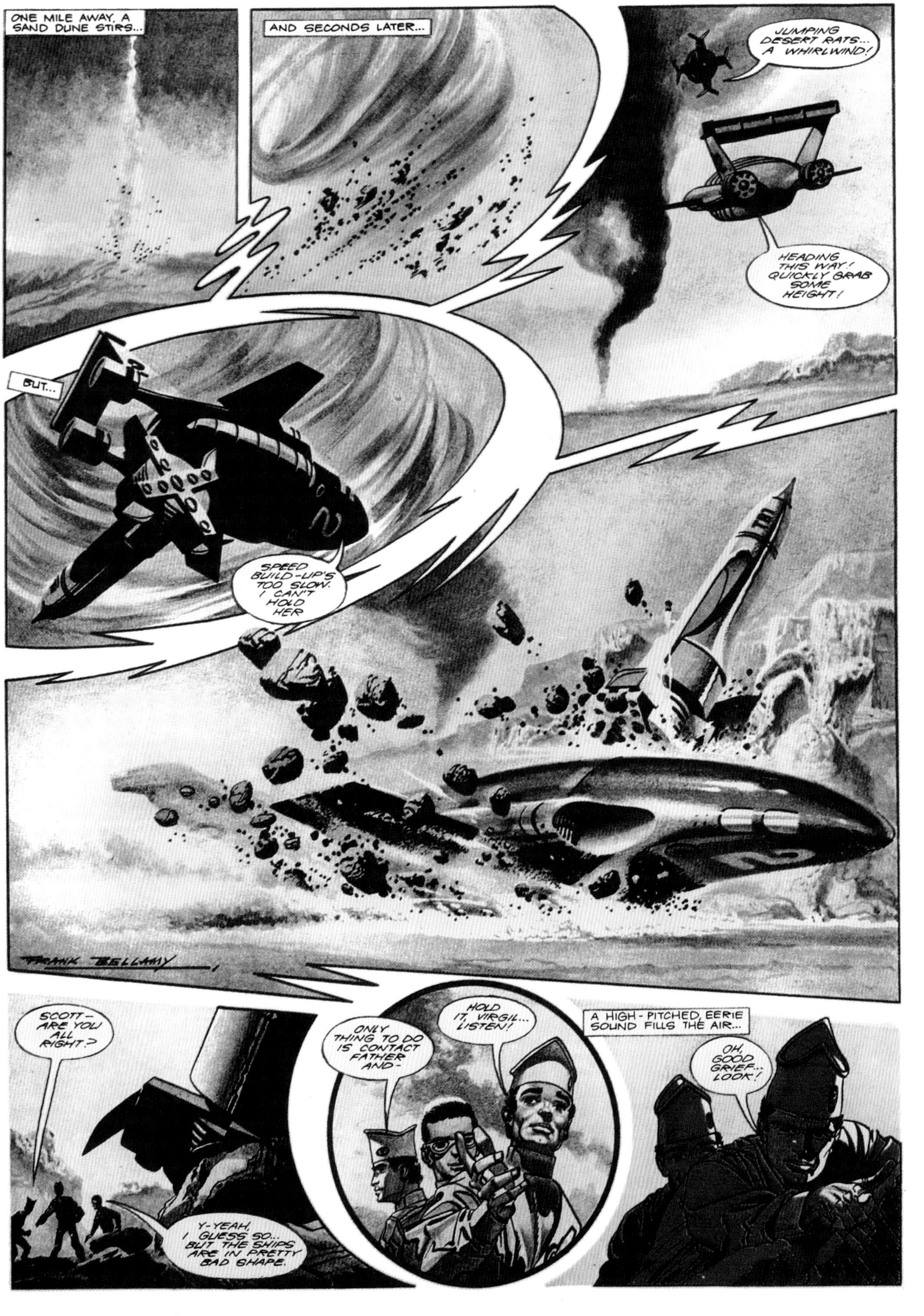
ONE MILE AWAY, A SAND DUNE STIRS...
AND SECONDS LATER...
JUMPING DESERT RATS... A WHIRLWIND!
HEADING THIS WAY! QUICKLY GRAB SOME HEIGHT!
BUT...
SPEED BUILD-UP'S TOO SLOW. I CAN'T HOLD HER
FRANK BELLAMY
SCOTT— ARE YOU ALL RIGHT?
Y-YEAH, I GUESS SO... BUT THE SHIPS ARE IN PRETTY BAD SHAPE.
ONLY THING TO DO IS CONTACT FATHER AND—
HOLD IT, VIRGIL... LISTEN!
A HIGH-PITCHED, EERIE SOUND FILLS THE AIR...
OH, GOOD GRIEF... LOOK!

Part 4 - dateline 21 October 2067

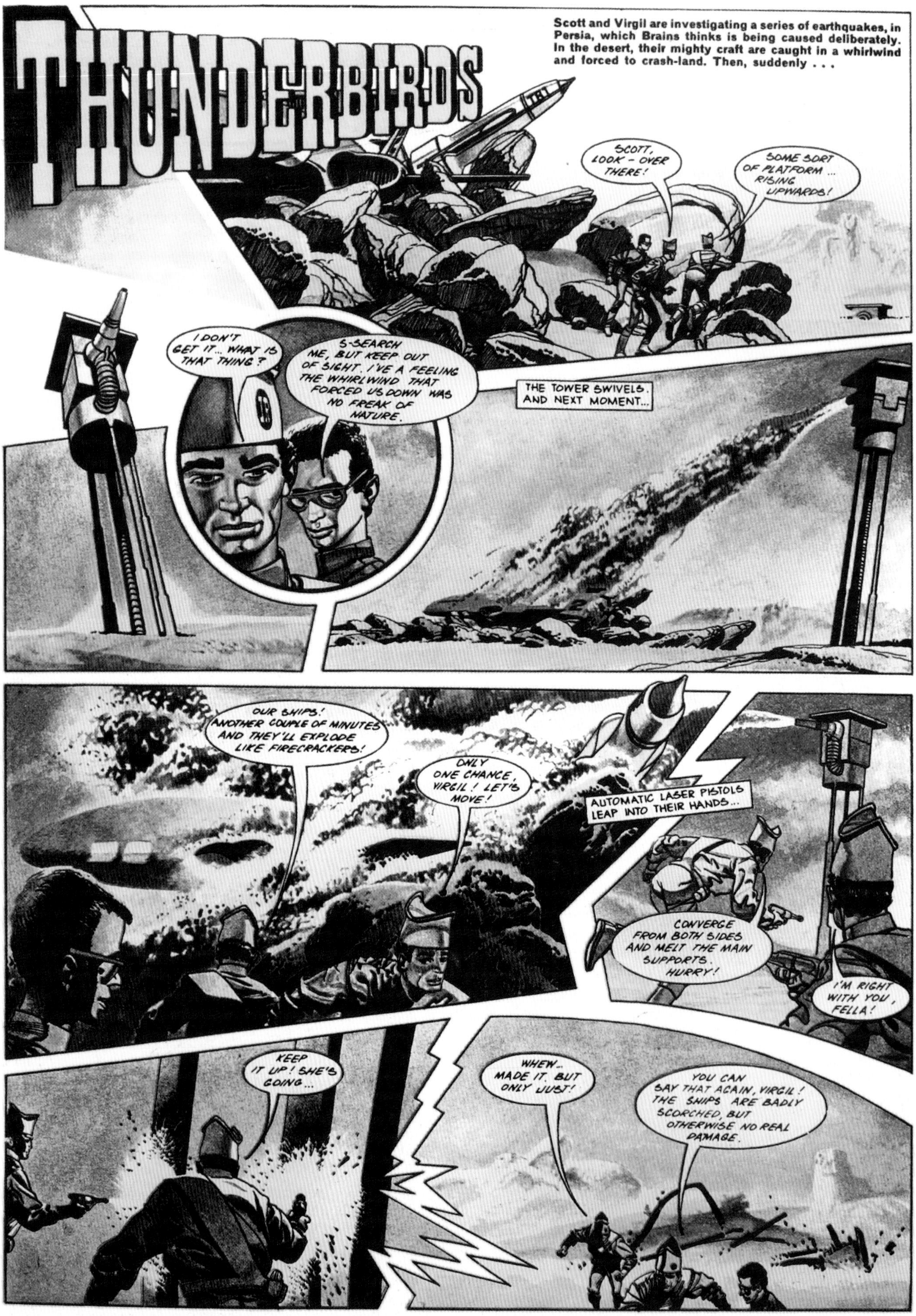
THUNDERBIRDS
Scott and Virgil are investigating a series of earthquakes, in Persia, which Brains thinks is being caused deliberately. In the desert, their mighty craft are caught in a whirlwind and forced to crash-land. Then, suddenly . . .
SCOTT, LOOK - OVER THERE!
SOME SORT OF PLATFORM ... RISING UPWARDS!
I DON'T GET IT... WHAT IS THAT THING?
S-SEARCH ME, BUT KEEP OUT OF SIGHT. I'VE A FEELING THE WHIRLWIND THAT FORCED US DOWN WAS NO FREAK OF NATURE.
THE TOWER SWIVELS. AND NEXT MOMENT...
OUR SHIPS! ANOTHER COUPLE OF MINUTES AND THEY'LL EXPLODE LIKE FIRECRACKERS!
ONLY ONE CHANCE, VIRGIL! LET'S MOVE!
AUTOMATIC LASER PISTOLS LEAP INTO THEIR HANDS...
CONVERGE FROM BOTH SIDES AND MELT THE MAIN SUPPORTS. HURRY!
I'M RIGHT WITH YOU, FELLA!
KEEP IT UP! SHE'S GOING...
WHEW... MADE IT. BUT ONLY JUST!
YOU CAN SAY THAT AGAIN, VIRGIL! THE SHIPS ARE BADLY SCORCHED, BUT OTHERWISE NO REAL DAMAGE.

Artist: Frank Bellamy

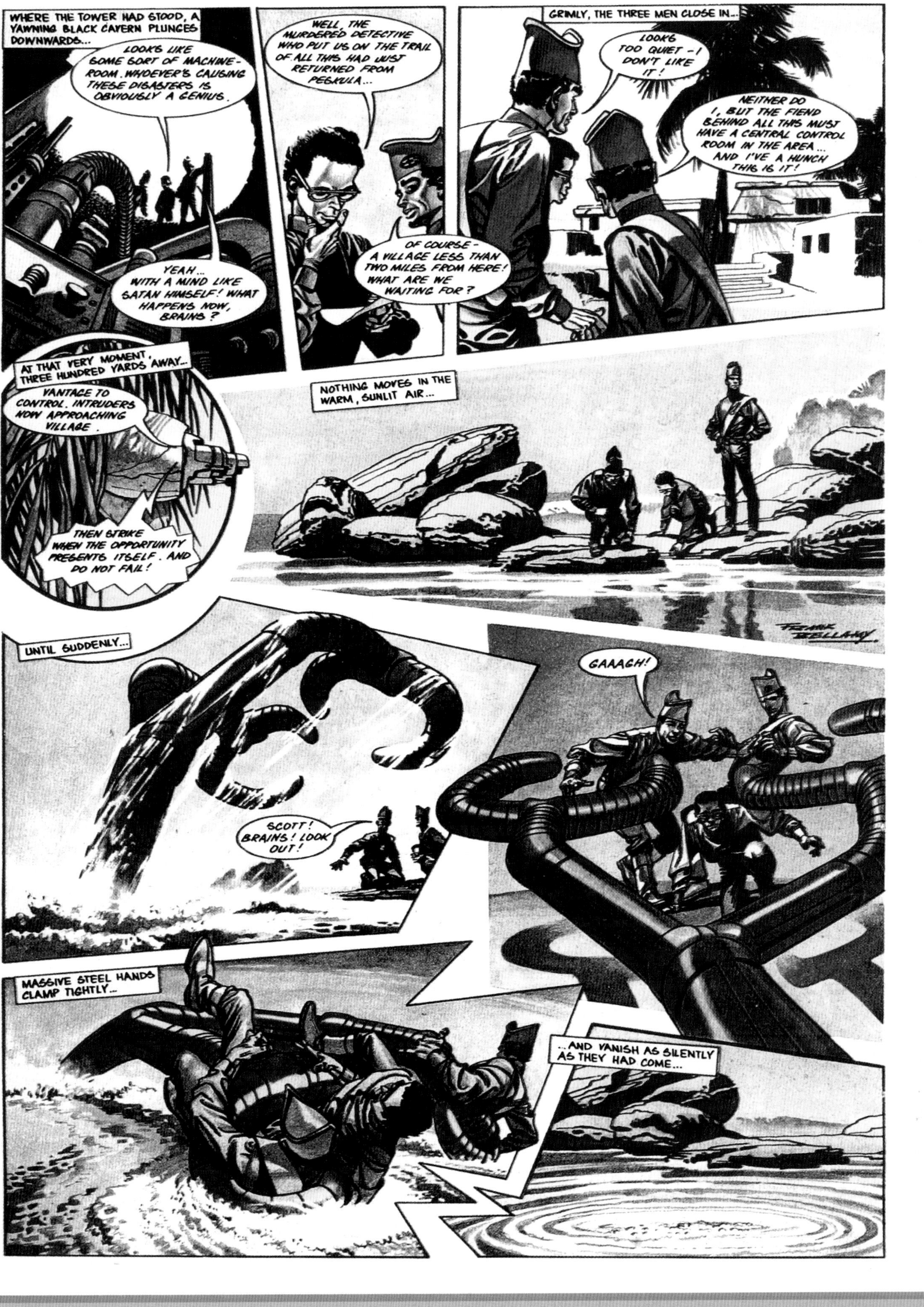

WHERE THE TOWER HAD STOOD, A YAWNING BLACK CAVERN PLUNGES DOWNWARDS...
LOOKS LIKE SOME SORT OF MACHINE-ROOM. WHOEVER'S CAUSING THESE DISASTERS IS OBVIOUSLY A GENIUS.
YEAH... WITH A MIND LIKE SATAN HIMSELF! WHAT HAPPENS NOW, BRAINS?
WELL, THE MURDERED DETECTIVE WHO PUT US ON THE TRAIL OF ALL THIS HAD JUST RETURNED FROM PESKULA...
OF COURSE - A VILLAGE LESS THAN TWO MILES FROM HERE! WHAT ARE WE WAITING FOR?
GRIMLY, THE THREE MEN CLOSE IN...
LOOKS TOO QUIET - I DON'T LIKE IT!
NEITHER DO I, BUT THE FIEND BEHIND ALL THIS MUST HAVE A CENTRAL CONTROL ROOM IN THE AREA... AND I'VE A HUNCH THIS IS IT!
AT THAT VERY MOMENT, THREE HUNDRED YARDS AWAY...
VANTAGE TO CONTROL. INTRUDERS NOW APPROACHING VILLAGE.
THEN STRIKE WHEN THE OPPORTUNITY PRESENTS ITSELF. AND DO NOT FAIL!
NOTHING MOVES IN THE WARM, SUNLIT AIR...
FRANK BELLAMY
UNTIL SUDDENLY...
SCOTT! BRAINS! LOOK OUT!
GAAAGH!
MASSIVE STEEL HANDS CLAMP TIGHTLY...
...AND VANISH AS SILENTLY AS THEY HAD COME...

Part 5 - dateline 28 October 2067

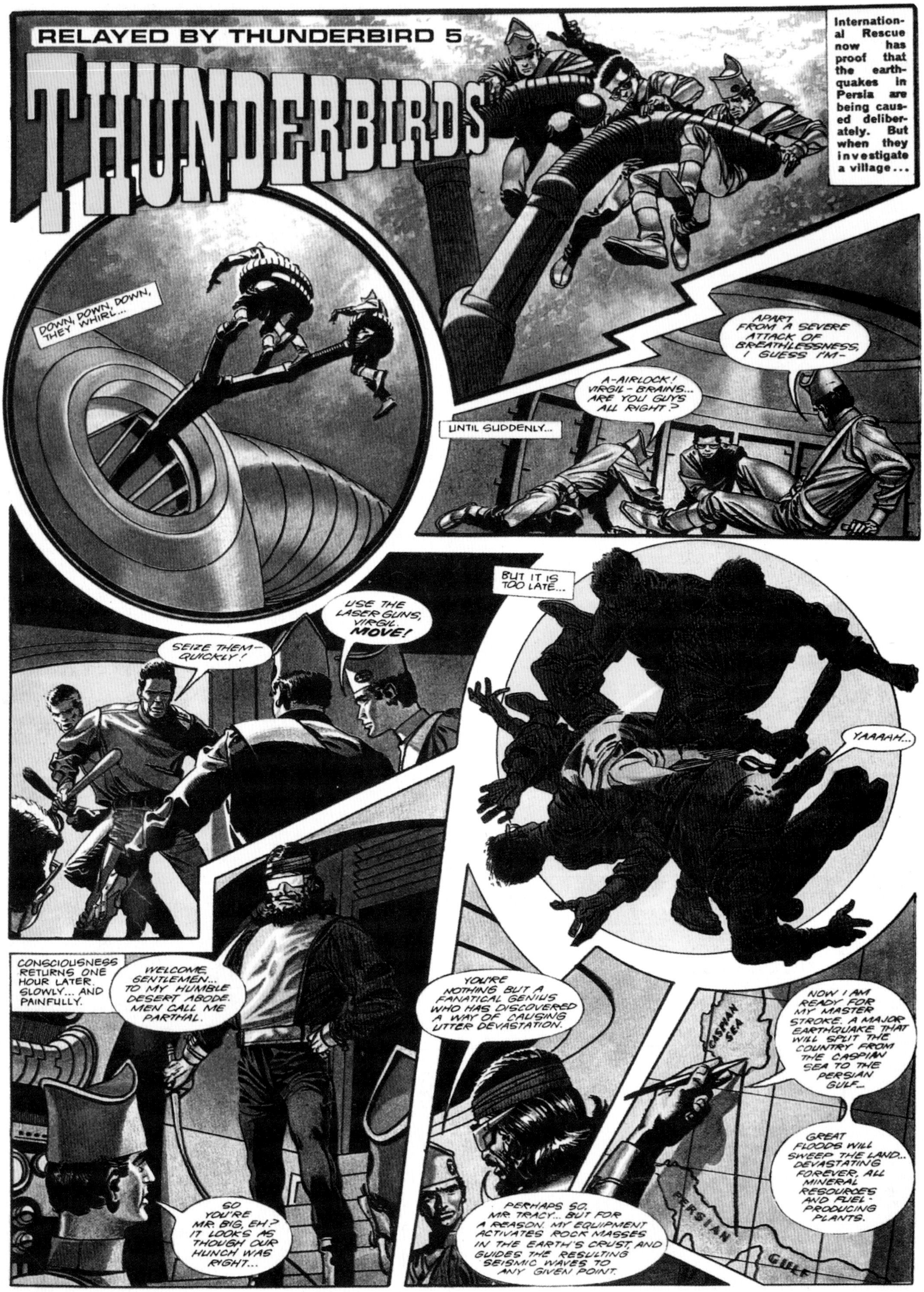
RELAYED BY THUNDERBIRD 5
THUNDERBIRDS
International Rescue now has proof that the earthquakes in Persia are being caused deliberately. But when they investigate a village . . .
DOWN, DOWN, DOWN, THEY WHIRL...
UNTIL SUDDENLY...
A-AIRLOCK! VIRGIL - BRAINS... ARE YOU GUYS ALL RIGHT?
APART FROM A SEVERE ATTACK OF BREATHLESSNESS, I GUESS I'M-
SEIZE THEM- QUICKLY!
USE THE LASER GUNS, VIRGIL. MOVE!
BUT IT IS TOO LATE...
YAAAAH...
CONSCIOUSNESS RETURNS ONE HOUR LATER. SLOWLY... AND PAINFULLY.
WELCOME, GENTLEMEN... TO MY HUMBLE DESERT ABODE. MEN CALL ME PARTHAL.
SO YOU'RE MR. BIG, EH? IT LOOKS AS THOUGH OUR HUNCH WAS RIGHT...
YOU'RE NOTHING BUT A FANATICAL GENIUS WHO HAS DISCOVERED A WAY OF CAUSING UTTER DEVASTATION.
PERHAPS SO, MR. TRACY... BUT FOR A REASON. MY EQUIPMENT ACTIVATES ROCK MASSES IN THE EARTH'S CRUST, AND GUIDES THE RESULTING SEISMIC WAVES TO ANY GIVEN POINT.
NOW I AM READY FOR MY MASTER STROKE. A MAJOR EARTHQUAKE THAT WILL SPLIT THE COUNTRY FROM THE CASPIAN SEA TO THE PERSIAN GULF...
GREAT FLOODS WILL SWEEP THE LAND... DEVASTATING FOREVER, ALL MINERAL RESOURCES AND FUEL-PRODUCING PLANTS.
CASPIAN SEA
PERSIAN GULF

Artist: Frank Bellamy

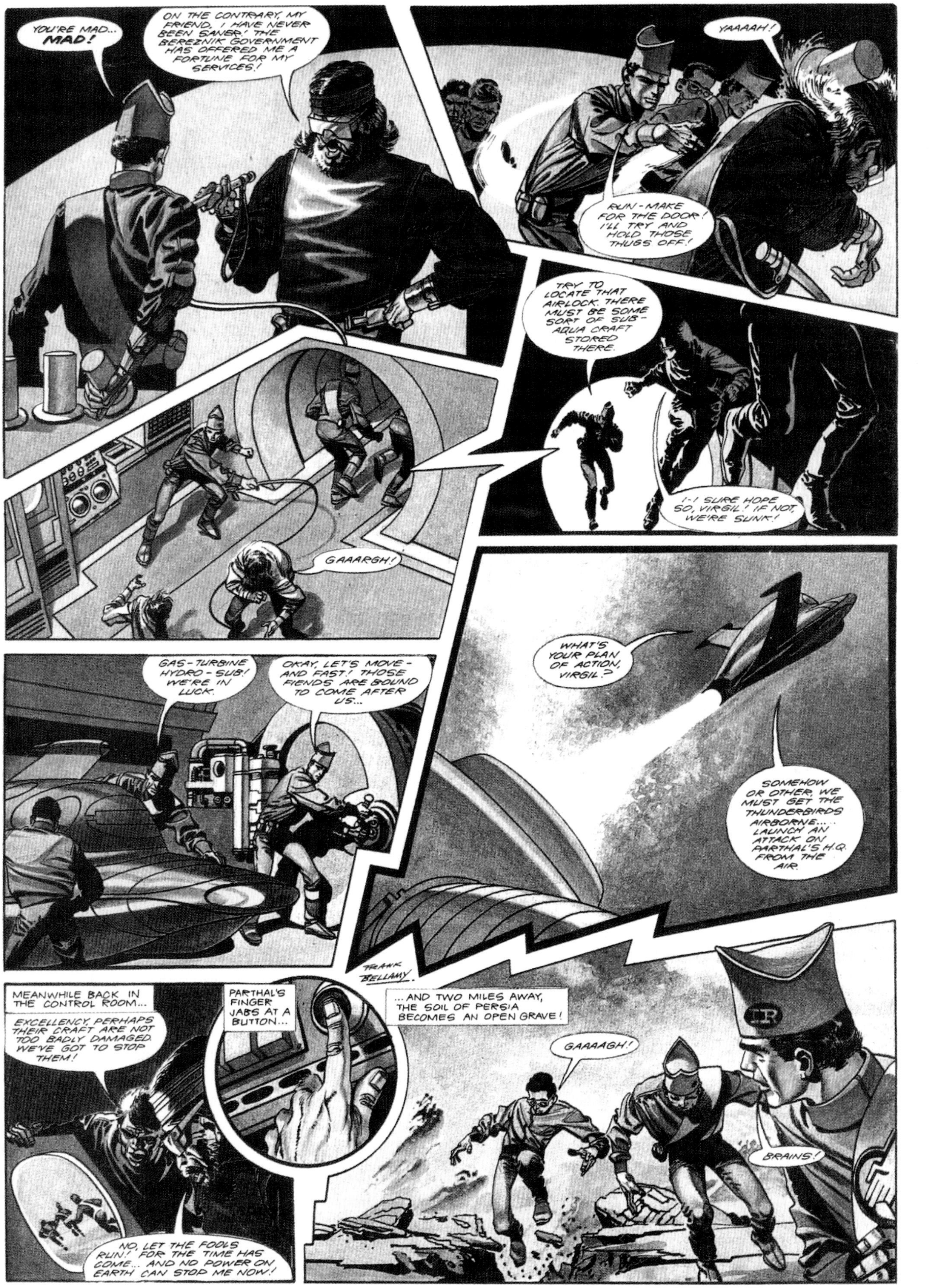
YOU'RE MAD... MAD!
ON THE CONTRARY, MY FRIEND, I HAVE NEVER BEEN SANER! THE BEREZNIK GOVERNMENT HAS OFFERED ME A FORTUNE FOR MY SERVICES!
YAAAAH!
RUN - MAKE FOR THE DOOR! I'LL TRY AND HOLD THOSE THUGS OFF!
TRY TO LOCATE THAT AIRLOCK. THERE MUST BE SOME SORT OF SUB-AQUA CRAFT STORED THERE.
I-I SURE HOPE SO, VIRGIL! IF NOT, WE'RE SUNK!
GAAARGH!
GAS-TURBINE HYDRO-SUB! WE'RE IN LUCK.
OKAY, LET'S MOVE - AND FAST! THOSE FIENDS ARE BOUND TO COME AFTER US...
WHAT'S YOUR PLAN OF ACTION, VIRGIL?
SOMEHOW OR OTHER, WE MUST GET THE THUNDERBIRDS AIRBORNE... LAUNCH AN ATTACK ON PARTHAL'S H.Q. FROM THE AIR.
FRANK BELLAMY.
MEANWHILE BACK IN THE CONTROL ROOM...
EXCELLENCY, PERHAPS THEIR CRAFT ARE NOT TOO BADLY DAMAGED. WE'VE GOT TO STOP THEM!
NO, LET THE FOOLS RUN! FOR THE TIME HAS COME... AND NO POWER ON EARTH CAN STOP ME NOW!
PARTHAL'S FINGER JABS AT A BUTTON...
...AND TWO MILES AWAY, THE SOIL OF PERSIA BECOMES AN OPEN GRAVE!
GAAAAGH!
BRAINS!

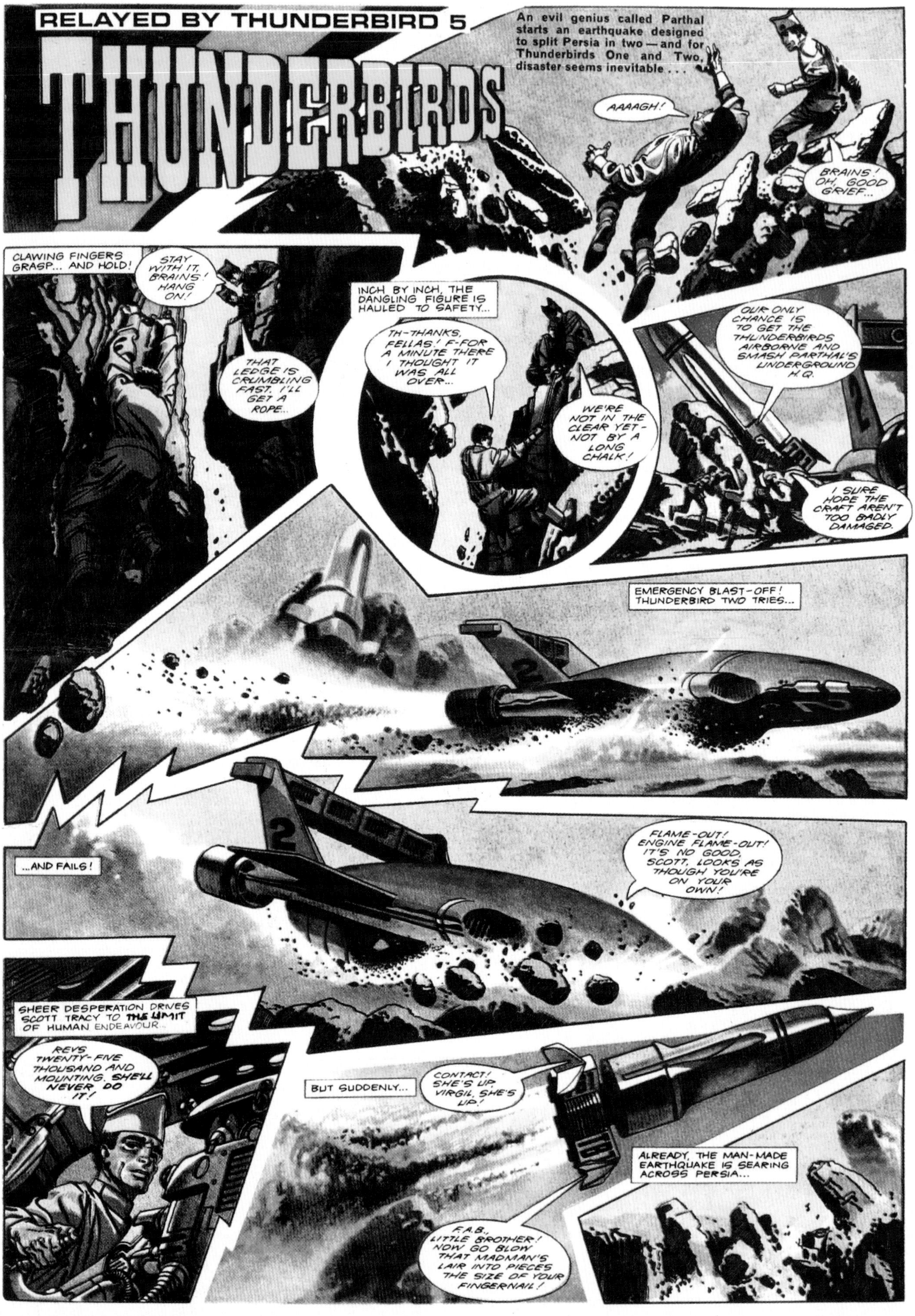
RELAYED BY THUNDERBIRD 5
THUNDERBIRDS
An evil genius called Parthal starts an earthquake designed to split Persia in two — and for Thunderbirds One and Two, disaster seems inevitable . . .
AAAAGH!
BRAINS! OH, GOOD GRIEF...
CLAWING FINGERS GRASP... AND HOLD!
STAY WITH IT, BRAINS! HANG ON!
THAT LEDGE IS CRUMBLING FAST. I'LL GET A ROPE...
INCH BY INCH, THE DANGLING FIGURE IS HAULED TO SAFETY...
TH-THANKS, FELLAS! F-FOR A MINUTE THERE I THOUGHT IT WAS ALL OVER...
WE'RE NOT IN THE CLEAR YET - NOT BY A LONG CHALK!
OUR ONLY CHANCE IS TO GET THE THUNDERBIRDS AIRBORNE AND SMASH PARTHAL'S UNDERGROUND H.Q.
I SURE HOPE THE CRAFT AREN'T TOO BADLY DAMAGED.
EMERGENCY BLAST-OFF! THUNDERBIRD TWO TRIES...
...AND FAILS!
FLAME-OUT! ENGINE FLAME-OUT! IT'S NO GOOD, SCOTT, LOOKS AS THOUGH YOU'RE ON YOUR OWN!
SHEER DESPERATION DRIVES SCOTT TRACY TO THE LIMIT OF HUMAN ENDEAVOUR...
REVS TWENTY-FIVE THOUSAND AND MOUNTING. SHE'LL NEVER DO IT!
BUT SUDDENLY...
CONTACT! SHE'S UP, VIRGIL, SHE'S UP!
ALREADY, THE MAN-MADE EARTHQUAKE IS SEARING ACROSS PERSIA...
F.A.B., LITTLE BROTHER! NOW GO BLOW THAT MADMAN'S LAIR INTO PIECES THE SIZE OF YOUR FINGERNAIL!

Part 6 - dateline 04 November 2067

Artist: Frank Bellamy

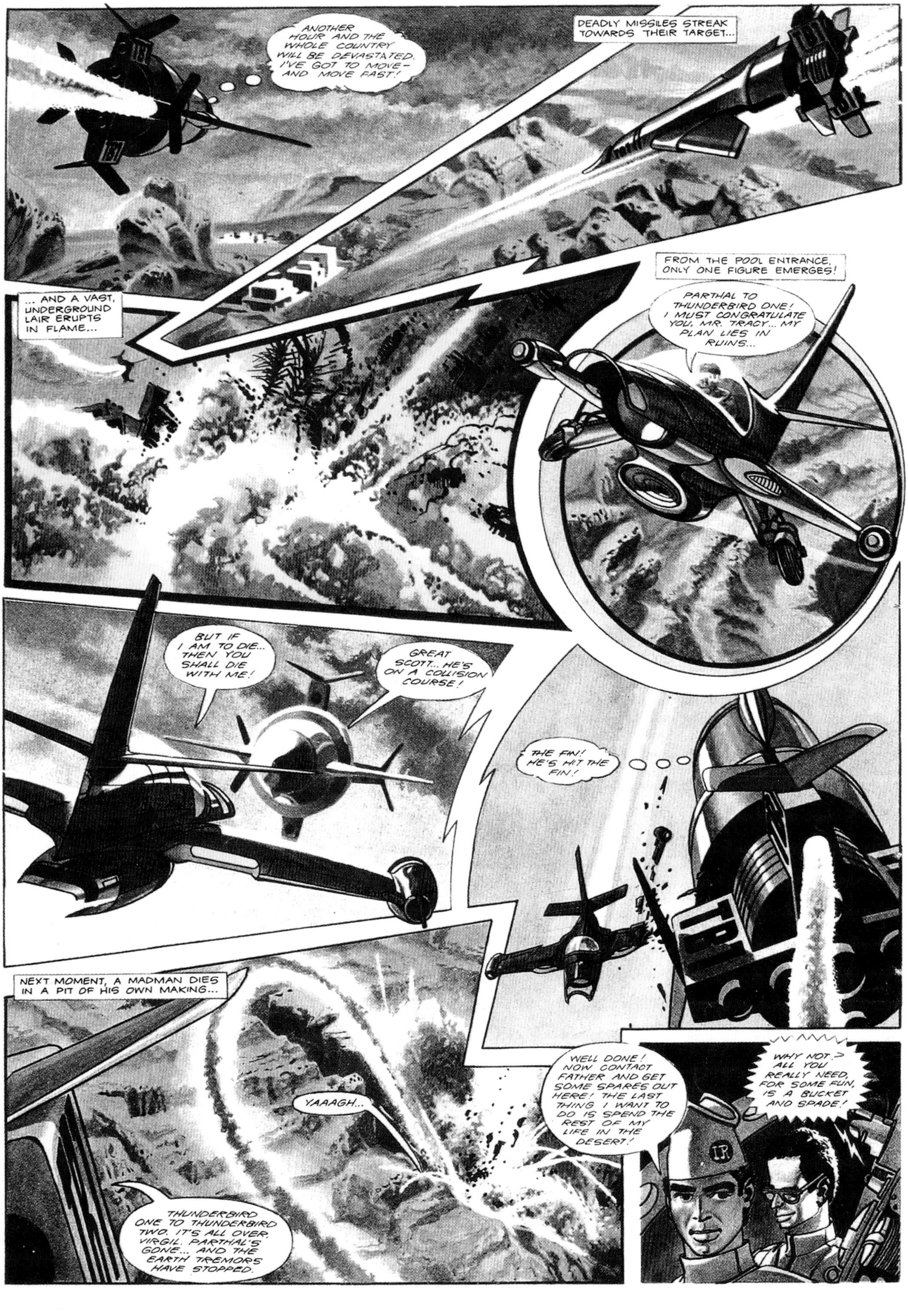
ANOTHER HOUR AND THE WHOLE COUNTRY WILL BE DEVASTATED. I'VE GOT TO MOVE - AND MOVE FAST!
DEADLY MISSILES STREAK TOWARDS THEIR TARGET...
... AND A VAST, UNDERGROUND LAIR ERUPTS IN FLAME...
FROM THE POOL ENTRANCE, ONLY ONE FIGURE EMERGES!
PARTHAL TO THUNDERBIRD ONE! I MUST CONGRATULATE YOU, MR. TRACY... MY PLAN LIES IN RUINS...
BUT IF I AM TO DIE... THEN YOU SHALL DIE WITH ME!
GREAT SCOTT... HE'S ON A COLLISION COURSE!
THE FIN! HE'S HIT THE FIN!
NEXT MOMENT, A MADMAN DIES IN A PIT OF HIS OWN MAKING...
YAAAGH...
THUNDERBIRD ONE TO THUNDERBIRD TWO. IT'S ALL OVER, VIRGIL. PARTHAL'S GONE... AND THE EARTH TREMORS HAVE STOPPED.
WELL DONE! NOW CONTACT FATHER AND GET SOME SPARES OUT HERE! THE LAST THING I WANT TO DO IS SPEND THE REST OF MY LIFE IN THE DESERT!
WHY NOT? ALL YOU REALLY NEED, FOR SOME FUN, IS A BUCKET AND SPADE!

Part 1 - dateline 11 November 2067

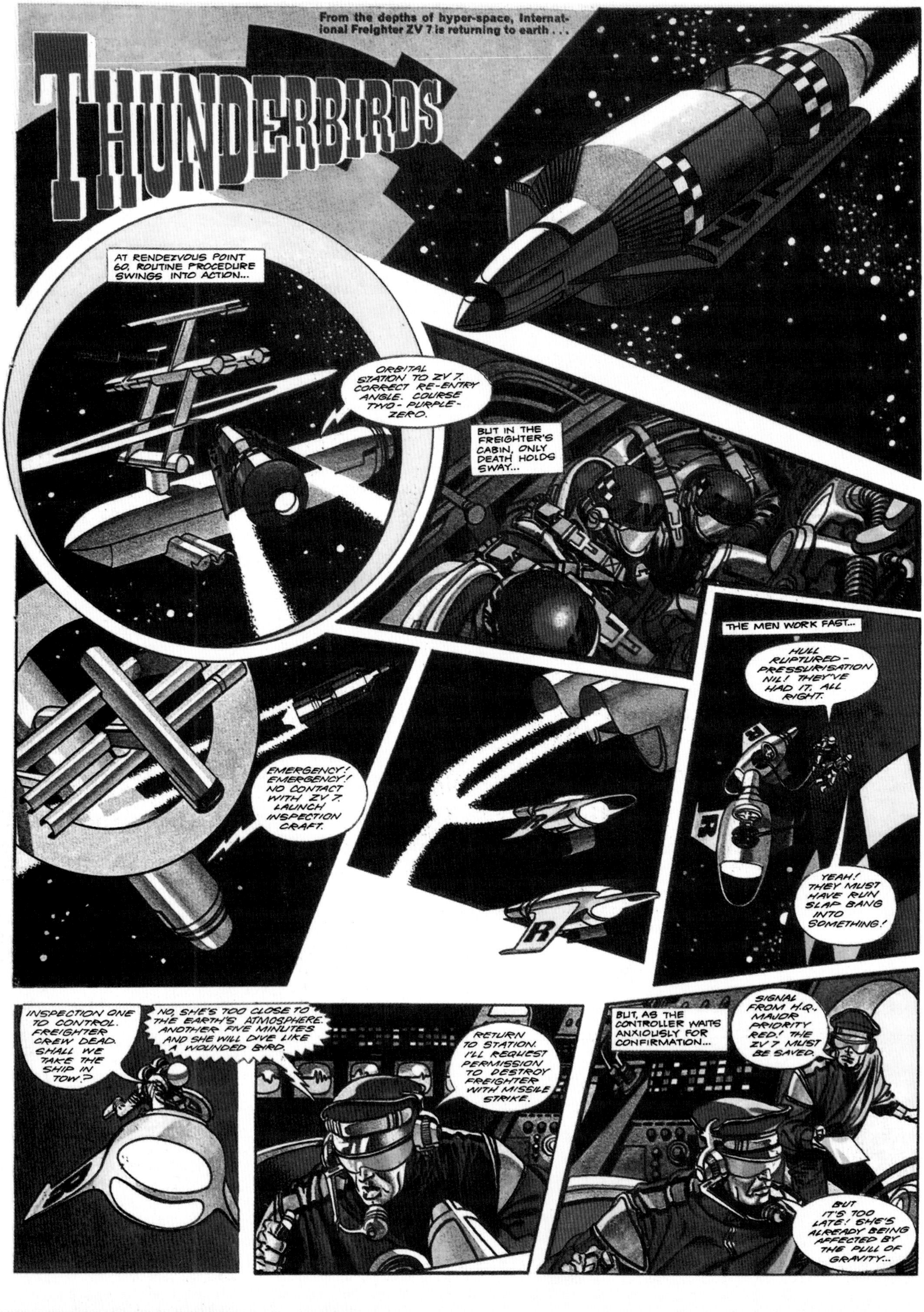
From the depths of hyper-space, International Freighter ZV 7 is returning to earth . . .
THUNDERBIRDS
AT RENDEZVOUS POINT 60, ROUTINE PROCEDURE SWINGS INTO ACTION...
ORBITAL STATION TO ZV 7. CORRECT RE-ENTRY ANGLE. COURSE TWO - PURPLE - ZERO.
BUT IN THE FREIGHTER'S CABIN, ONLY DEATH HOLDS SWAY...
EMERGENCY! EMERGENCY! NO CONTACT WITH ZV 7. LAUNCH INSPECTION CRAFT.
THE MEN WORK FAST...
HULL RUPTURED - PRESSURISATION NIL! THEY'VE HAD IT, ALL RIGHT.
YEAH! THEY MUST HAVE RUN SLAP BANG INTO SOMETHING!
INSPECTION ONE TO CONTROL. FREIGHTER CREW DEAD. SHALL WE TAKE THE SHIP IN TOW?
NO, SHE'S TOO CLOSE TO THE EARTH'S ATMOSPHERE. ANOTHER FIVE MINUTES AND SHE WILL DIVE LIKE A WOUNDED BIRD.
RETURN TO STATION. I'LL REQUEST PERMISSION TO DESTROY FREIGHTER WITH MISSILE STRIKE.
BUT, AS THE CONTROLLER WAITS ANXIOUSLY FOR CONFIRMATION...
SIGNAL FROM H.Q. MAJOR PRIORITY RED! THE ZV 7 MUST BE SAVED.
BUT IT'S TOO LATE! SHE'S ALREADY BEING AFFECTED BY THE PULL OF GRAVITY...

Artist: Frank Bellamy

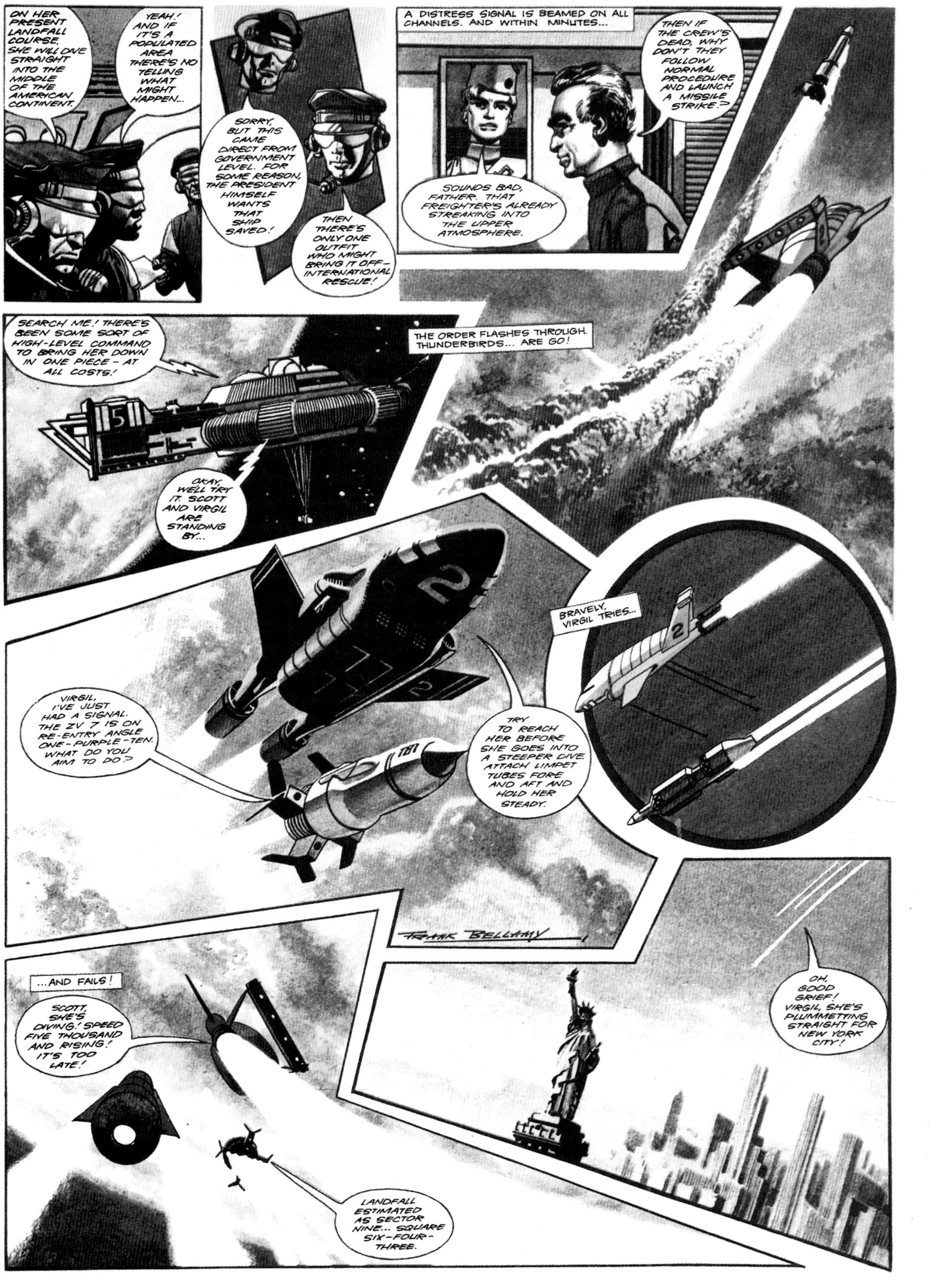
ON HER PRESENT LANDFALL COURSE, SHE WILL DIVE STRAIGHT INTO THE MIDDLE OF THE AMERICAN CONTINENT.
YEAH! AND IF IT'S A POPULATED AREA THERE'S NO TELLING WHAT MIGHT HAPPEN...
SORRY, BUT THIS CAME DIRECT FROM GOVERNMENT LEVEL. FOR SOME REASON, THE PRESIDENT HIMSELF WANTS THAT SHIP SAVED!
THEN THERE'S ONLY ONE OUTFIT WHO MIGHT BRING IT OFF– INTERNATIONAL RESCUE!
A DISTRESS SIGNAL IS BEAMED ON ALL CHANNELS. AND WITHIN MINUTES...
THEN IF THE CREW'S DEAD, WHY DON'T THEY FOLLOW NORMAL PROCEDURE AND LAUNCH A MISSILE STRIKE?
SOUNDS BAD, FATHER. THAT FREIGHTER'S ALREADY STREAKING INTO THE UPPER ATMOSPHERE.
SEARCH ME! THERE'S BEEN SOME SORT OF HIGH-LEVEL COMMAND TO BRING HER DOWN IN ONE PIECE – AT ALL COSTS!
OKAY, WELL TRY IT. SCOTT AND VIRGIL ARE STANDING BY...
THE ORDER FLASHES THROUGH. THUNDERBIRDS... ARE GO!
VIRGIL, I'VE JUST HAD A SIGNAL. THE ZV 7 IS ON RE-ENTRY ANGLE ONE-PURPLE-TEN. WHAT DO YOU AIM TO DO?
TRY TO REACH HER BEFORE SHE GOES INTO A STEEPER DIVE. ATTACH LIMPET TUBES FORE AND AFT AND HOLD HER STEADY.
BRAVELY, VIRGIL TRIES...
FRANK BELLAMY
...AND FAILS!
SCOTT, SHE'S DIVING! SPEED FIVE THOUSAND AND RISING! IT'S TOO LATE!
LANDFALL ESTIMATED AS SECTOR NINE... SQUARE SIX-FOUR-THREE.
OH, GOOD GRIEF! VIRGIL, SHE'S PLUMMETTING STRAIGHT FOR NEW YORK CITY!

Part 2 - dateline 18 November 2067

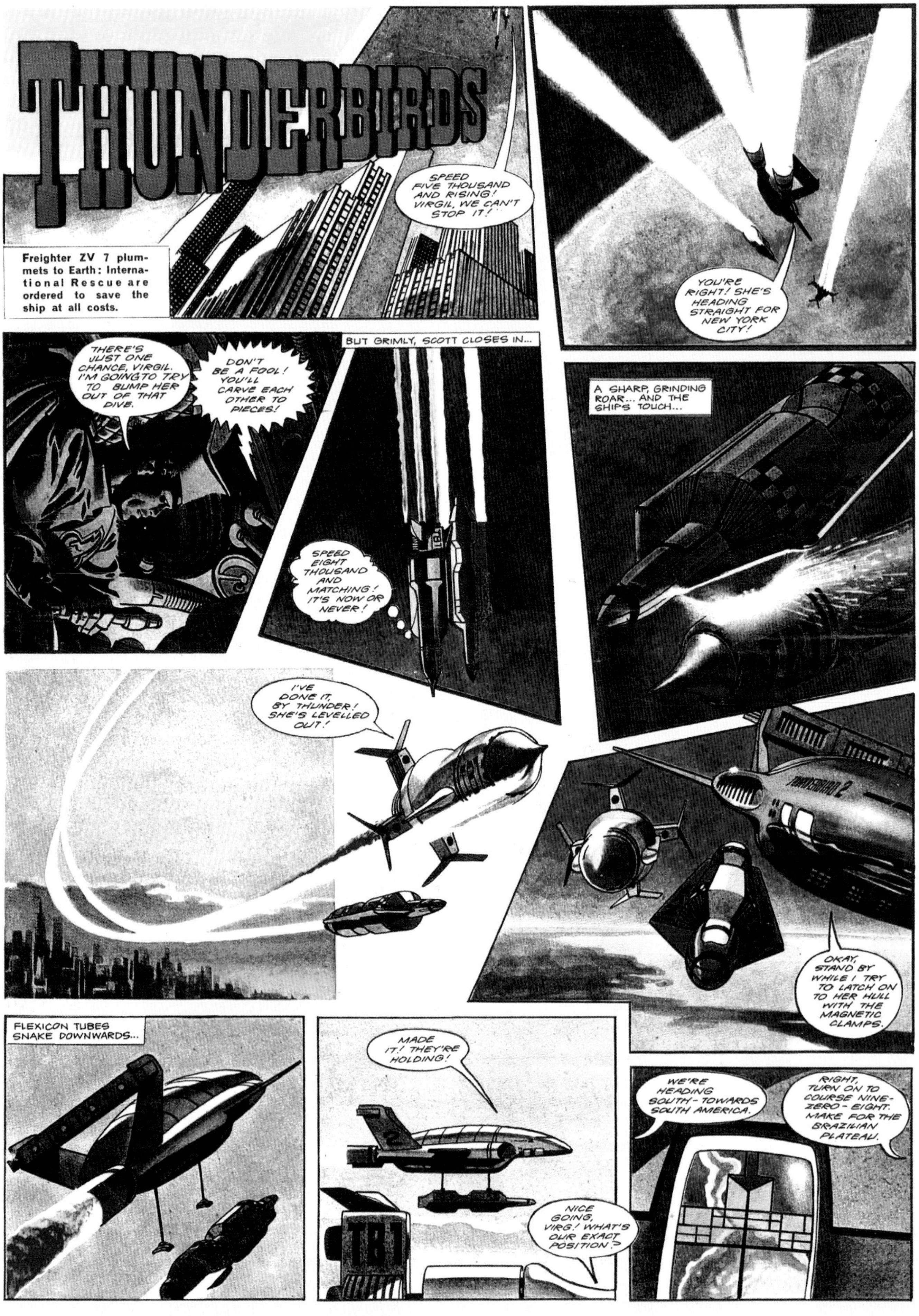
THUNDERBIRDS
Freighter ZV 7 plummets to Earth: International Rescue are ordered to save the ship at all costs.
SPEED FIVE THOUSAND AND RISING! VIRGIL, WE CAN'T STOP IT!
YOU'RE RIGHT! SHE'S HEADING STRAIGHT FOR NEW YORK CITY!
THERE'S JUST ONE CHANCE, VIRGIL. I'M GOING TO TRY TO BUMP HER OUT OF THAT DIVE.
DON'T BE A FOOL! YOU'LL CARVE EACH OTHER TO PIECES!
BUT GRIMLY, SCOTT CLOSES IN...
SPEED EIGHT THOUSAND AND MATCHING! IT'S NOW OR NEVER!
A SHARP, GRINDING ROAR... AND THE SHIPS TOUCH...
I'VE DONE IT, BY THUNDER! SHE'S LEVELLED OUT!
OKAY, STAND BY WHILE I TRY TO LATCH ON TO HER HULL WITH THE MAGNETIC CLAMPS.
FLEXICON TUBES SNAKE DOWNWARDS...
MADE IT! THEY'RE HOLDING!
NICE GOING, VIRG! WHAT'S OUR EXACT POSITION?
WE'RE HEADING SOUTH - TOWARDS SOUTH AMERICA.
RIGHT, TURN ON TO COURSE NINE-ZERO - EIGHT. MAKE FOR THE BRAZILIAN PLATEAU.

Artist: Frank Bellamy

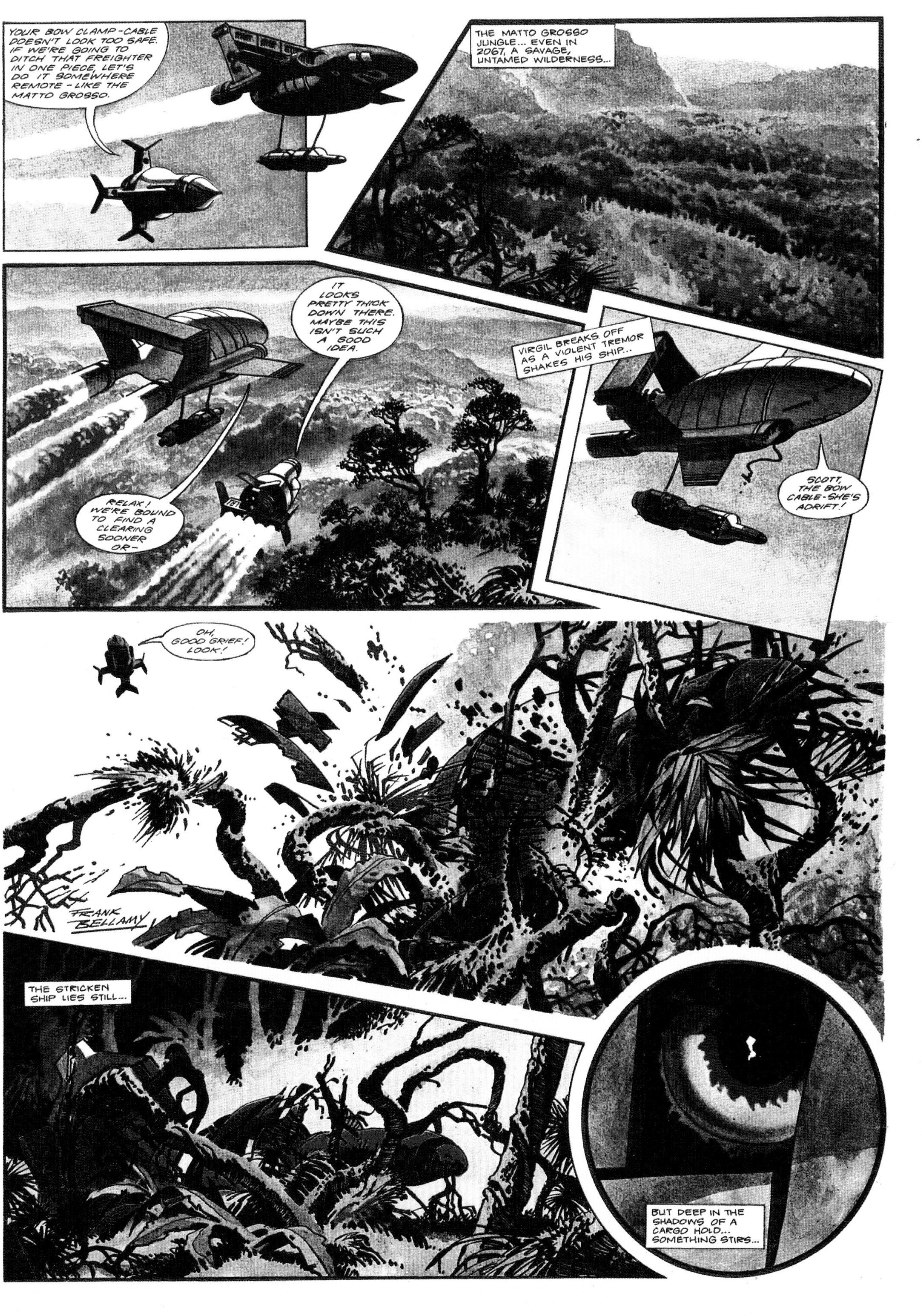
YOUR BOW CLAMP-CABLE DOESN'T LOOK TOO SAFE. IF WE'RE GOING TO DITCH THAT FREIGHTER IN ONE PIECE, LET'S DO IT SOMEWHERE REMOTE - LIKE THE MATTO GROSSO.
THE MATTO GROSSO JUNGLE... EVEN IN 2067, A SAVAGE, UNTAMED WILDERNESS...
IT LOOKS PRETTY THICK DOWN THERE. MAYBE THIS ISN'T SUCH A GOOD IDEA.
RELAX! WE'RE BOUND TO FIND A CLEARING SOONER OR-
VIRGIL BREAKS OFF AS A VIOLENT TREMOR SHAKES HIS SHIP...
SCOTT, THE BOW CABLE-SHE'S ADRIFT!
OH, GOOD GRIEF! LOOK!
FRANK BELLAMY
THE STRICKEN SHIP LIES STILL...
BUT DEEP IN THE SHADOWS OF A CARGO HOLD... SOMETHING STIRS...

Part 3 - dateline 25 November 2067

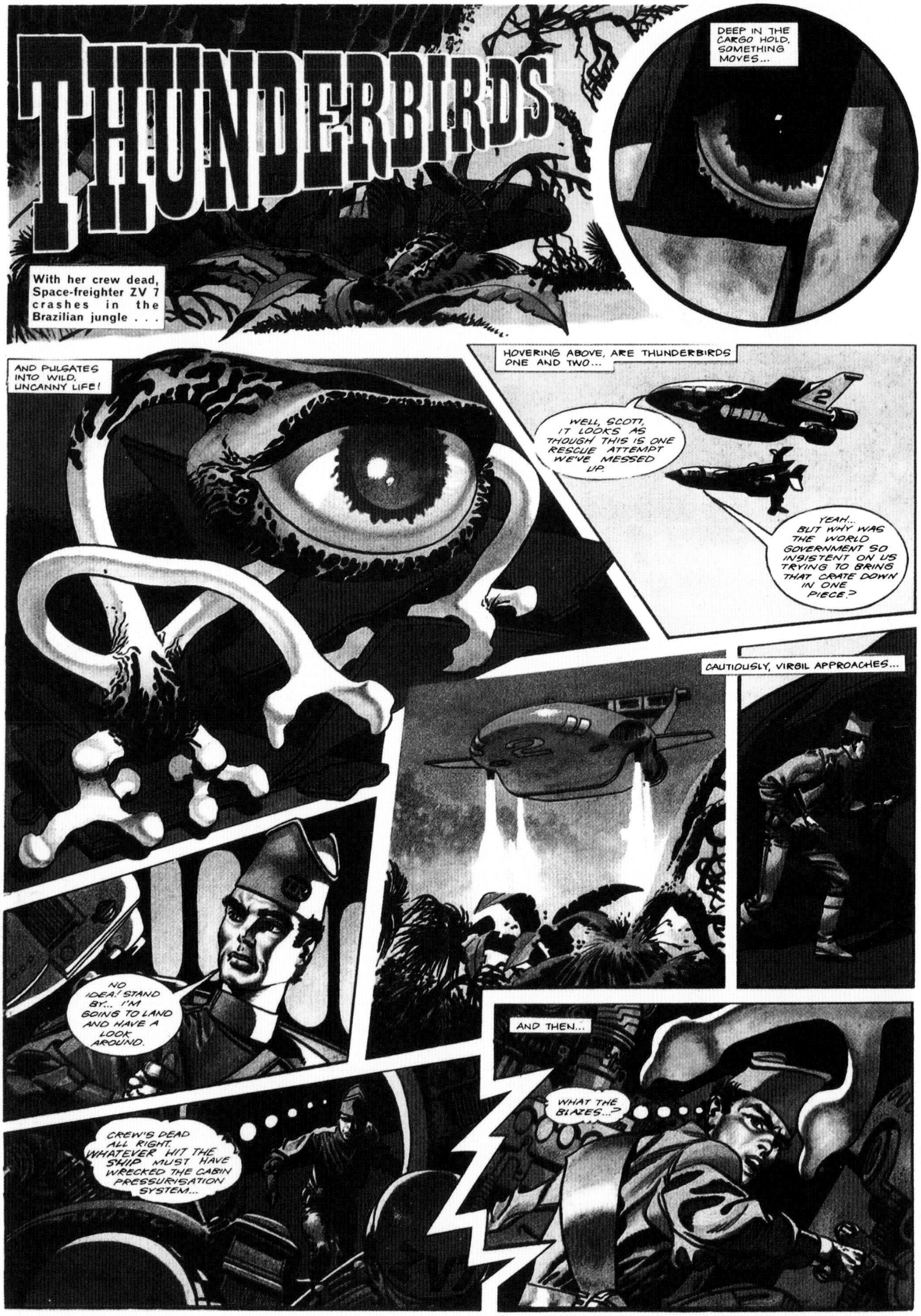
THUNDERBIRDS
With her crew dead, Space-freighter ZV 7 crashes in the Brazilian jungle . . .
DEEP IN THE CARGO HOLD, SOMETHING MOVES...
AND PULSATES INTO WILD, UNCANNY LIFE!
HOVERING ABOVE, ARE THUNDERBIRDS ONE AND TWO...
WELL, SCOTT, IT LOOKS AS THOUGH THIS IS ONE RESCUE ATTEMPT WE'VE MESSED UP.
YEAH... BUT WHY WAS THE WORLD GOVERNMENT SO INSISTENT ON US TRYING TO BRING THAT CRATE DOWN IN ONE PIECE?
NO IDEA! STAND BY... I'M GOING TO LAND AND HAVE A LOOK AROUND.
CAUTIOUSLY, VIRGIL APPROACHES...
CREW'S DEAD ALL RIGHT. WHATEVER HIT THE SHIP MUST HAVE WRECKED THE CABIN PRESSURISATION SYSTEM...
AND THEN...
WHAT THE BLAZES...?

Artist: Frank Bellamy

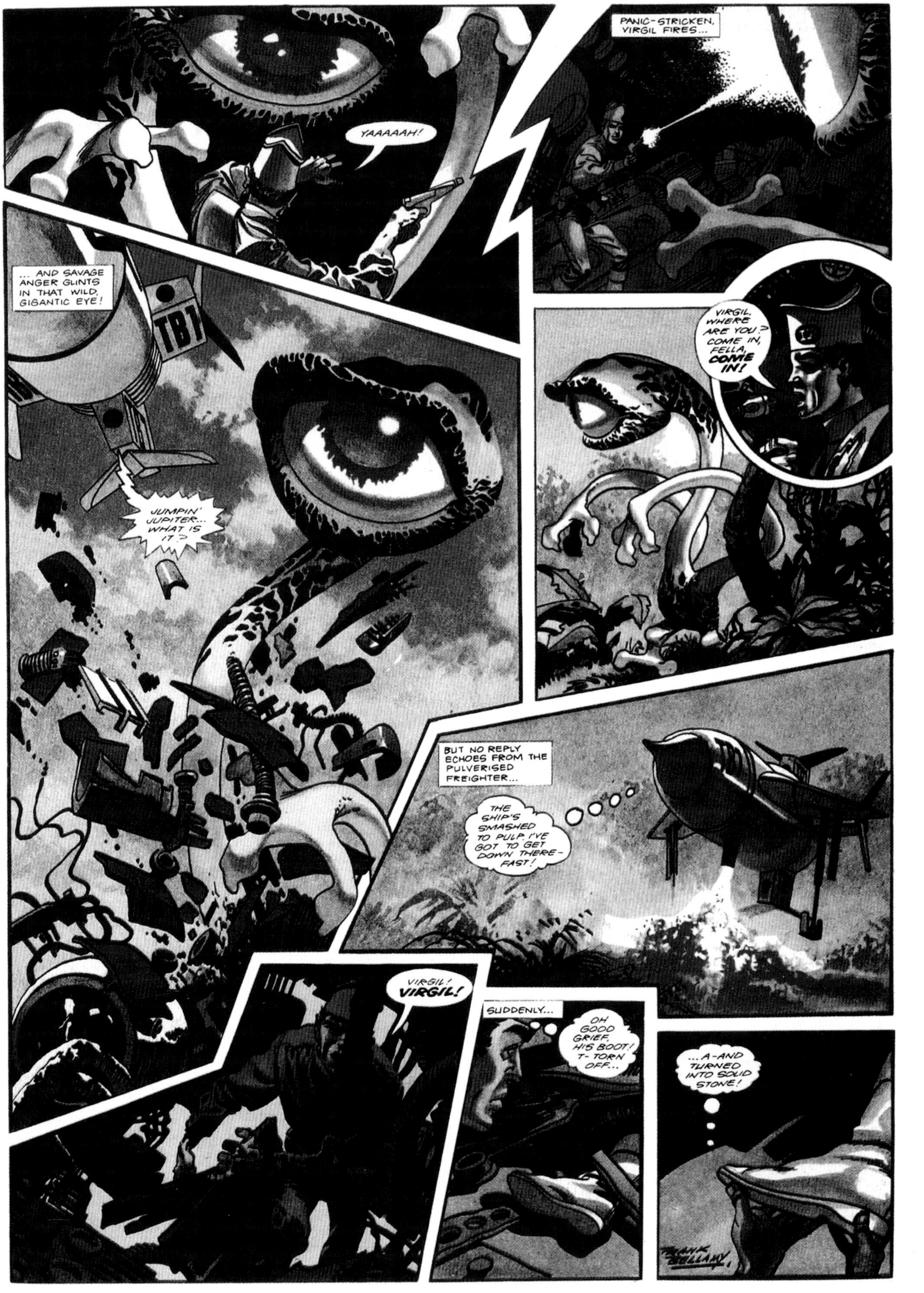
YAAAAAH!
PANIC-STRICKEN, VIRGIL FIRES...
... AND SAVAGE ANGER GLINTS IN THAT WILD, GIGANTIC EYE!
TB1
JUMPIN' JUPITER... WHAT IS IT?
VIRGIL, WHERE ARE YOU? COME IN, FELLA, COME IN!
BUT NO REPLY ECHOES FROM THE PULVERISED FREIGHTER...
THE SHIP'S SMASHED TO PULP. I'VE GOT TO GET DOWN THERE-FAST!
VIRGIL! VIRGIL!
SUDDENLY...
OH GOOD GRIEF. HIS BOOT! T-TORN OFF...
... A-AND TURNED INTO SOLID STONE!
FRANK BELLAMY

Part 4 - dateline 02 December 2067

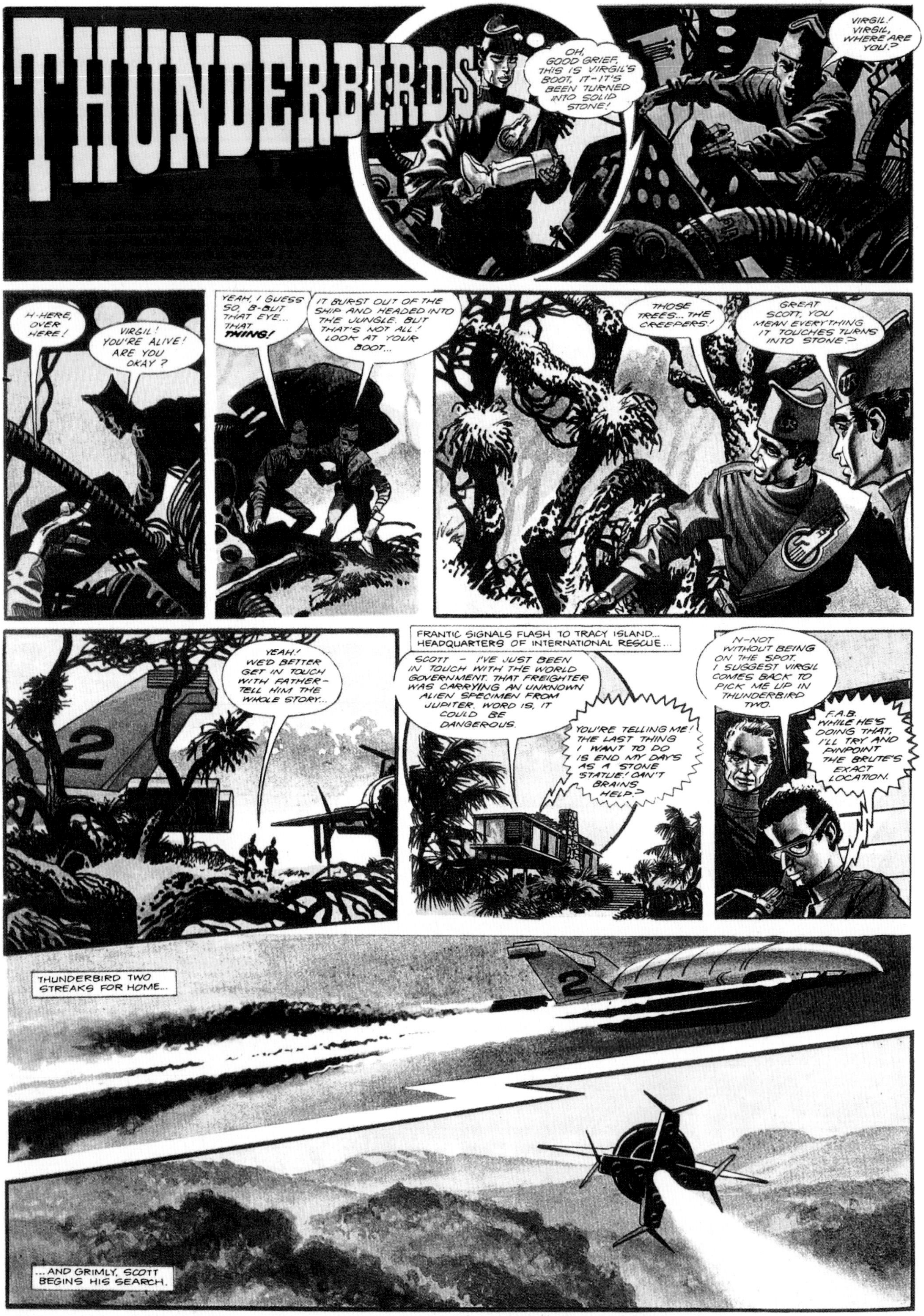
THUNDERBIRDS
OH, GOOD GRIEF, THIS IS VIRGIL'S BOOT, IT–IT'S BEEN TURNED INTO SOLID STONE!
VIRGIL! VIRGIL, WHERE ARE YOU?
H-HERE, OVER HERE!
VIRGIL! YOU'RE ALIVE! ARE YOU OKAY?
YEAH, I GUESS SO, B-BUT THAT EYE... THAT THING!
IT BURST OUT OF THE SHIP AND HEADED INTO THE JUNGLE. BUT THAT'S NOT ALL! LOOK AT YOUR BOOT...
THOSE TREES... THE CREEPERS!
GREAT SCOTT, YOU MEAN EVERYTHING IT TOUCHES TURNS INTO STONE?
YEAH! WE'D BETTER GET IN TOUCH WITH FATHER– TELL HIM THE WHOLE STORY...
FRANTIC SIGNALS FLASH TO TRACY ISLAND... HEADQUARTERS OF INTERNATIONAL RESCUE...
SCOTT – I'VE JUST BEEN IN TOUCH WITH THE WORLD GOVERNMENT. THAT FREIGHTER WAS CARRYING AN UNKNOWN ALIEN SPECIMEN FROM JUPITER. WORD IS, IT COULD BE DANGEROUS.
YOU'RE TELLING ME! THE LAST THING I WANT TO DO IS END MY DAYS AS A STONE 'STATUE'! CAN'T BRAINS HELP?
N-NOT WITHOUT BEING ON THE SPOT. I SUGGEST VIRGIL COMES BACK TO PICK ME UP IN THUNDERBIRD TWO.
F.A.B. WHILE HE'S DOING THAT, I'LL TRY AND PINPOINT THE BRUTE'S EXACT LOCATION.
THUNDERBIRD TWO STREAKS FOR HOME...
...AND GRIMLY, SCOTT BEGINS HIS SEARCH.

Artist: Frank Bellamy

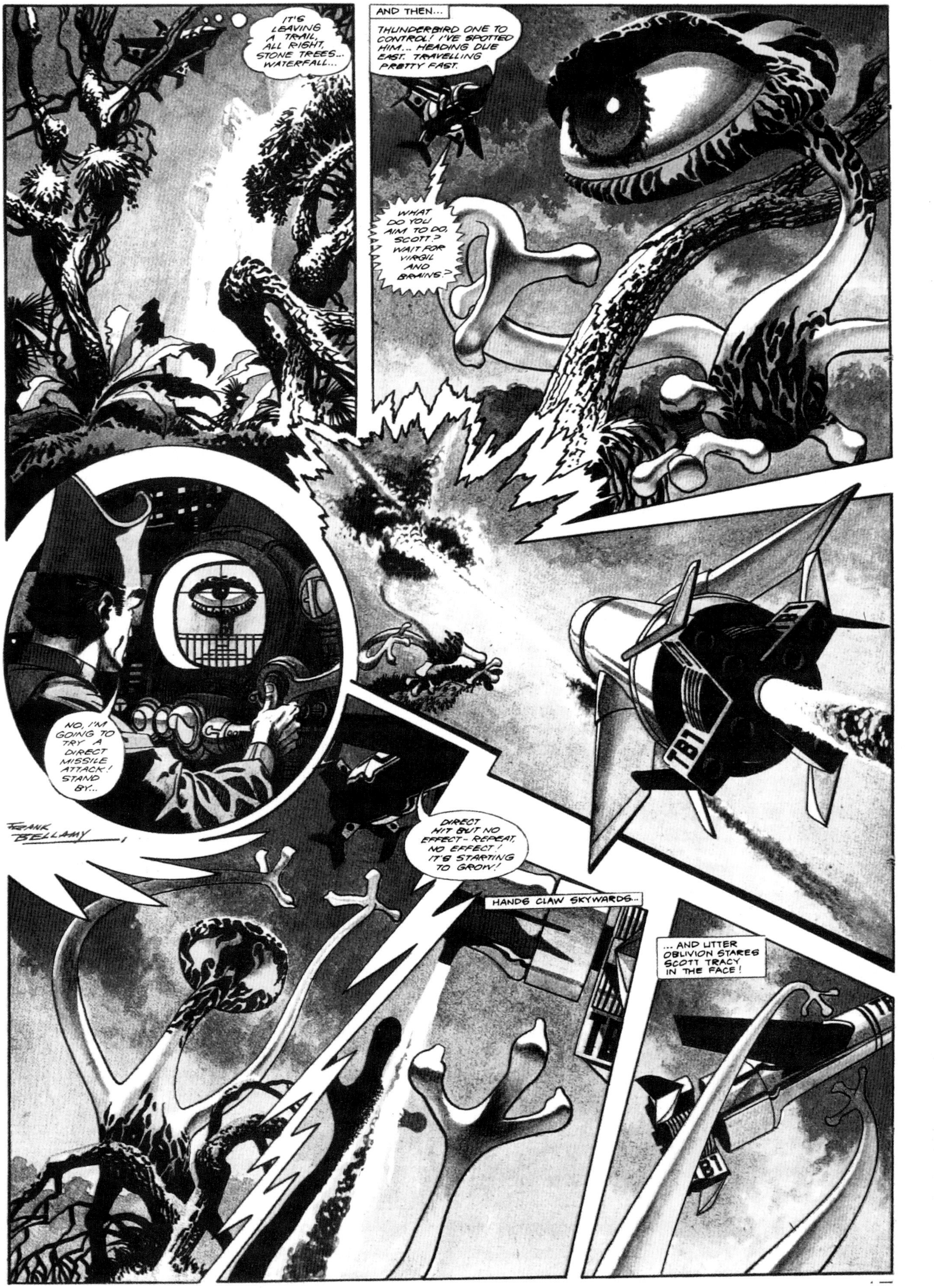
IT'S LEAVING A TRAIL, ALL RIGHT, STONE TREES... WATERFALL...
AND THEN...
THUNDERBIRD ONE TO CONTROL! I'VE SPOTTED HIM... HEADING DUE EAST. TRAVELLING PRETTY FAST.
WHAT DO YOU AIM TO DO, SCOTT? WAIT FOR VIRGIL AND BRAINS?
NO, I'M GOING TO TRY A DIRECT MISSILE ATTACK! STAND BY...
TB1
FRANK BELLAMY
DIRECT HIT BUT NO EFFECT- REPEAT, NO EFFECT! IT'S STARTING TO GROW!
HANDS CLAW SKYWARDS...
... AND UTTER OBLIVION STARES SCOTT TRACY IN THE FACE!

Part 5 - dateline 09 December 2067

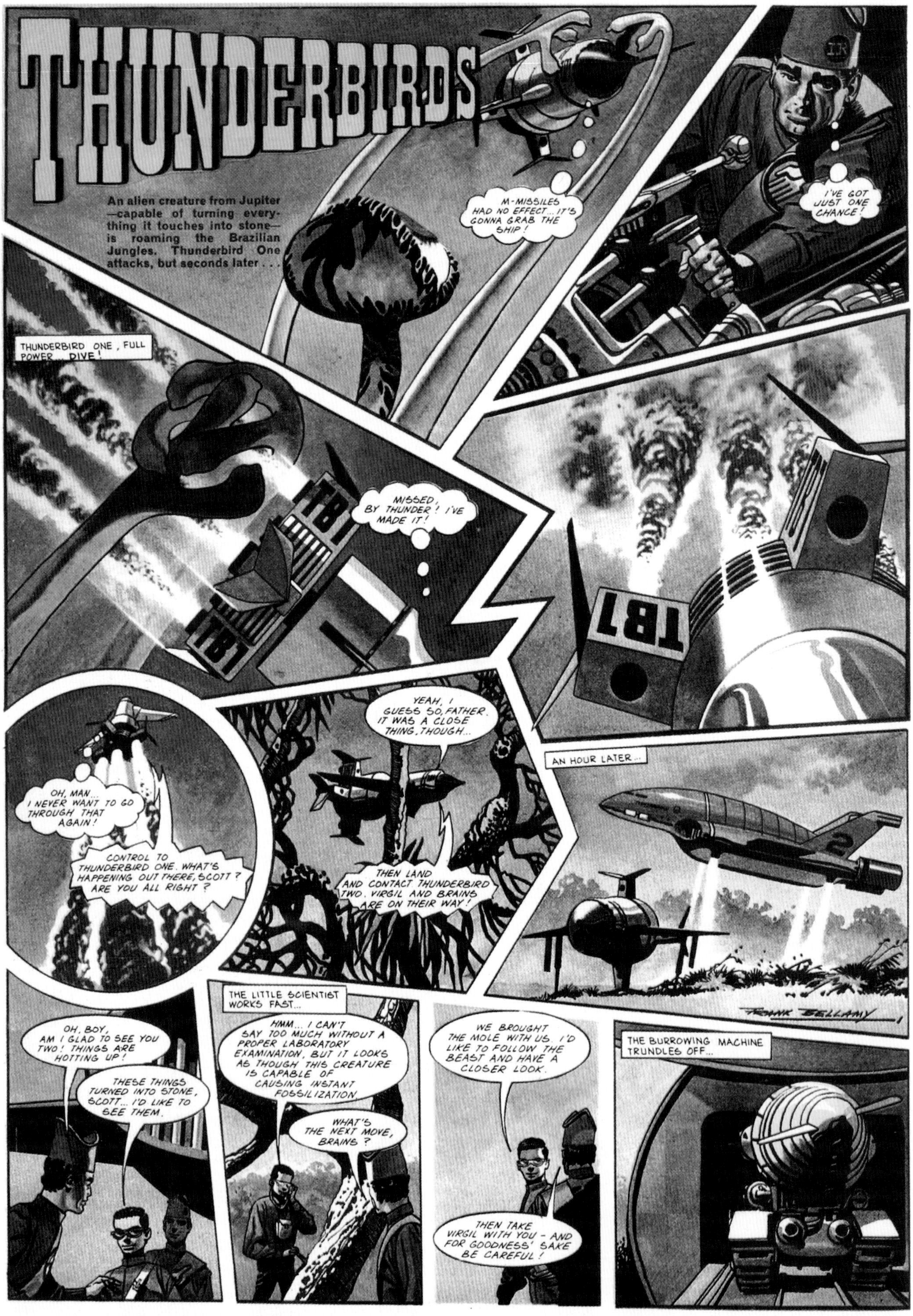
THUNDERBIRDS
An alien creature from Jupiter —capable of turning everything it touches into stone— is roaming the Brazilian Jungles. Thunderbird One attacks, but seconds later . . .
M-MISSILES HAD NO EFFECT... IT'S GONNA GRAB THE SHIP!
I'VE GOT JUST ONE CHANCE!
THUNDERBIRD ONE, FULL POWER... DIVE!
TB1
MISSED, BY THUNDER! I'VE MADE IT!
TB1
OH, MAN... I NEVER WANT TO GO THROUGH THAT AGAIN!
CONTROL TO THUNDERBIRD ONE. WHAT'S HAPPENING OUT THERE, SCOTT? ARE YOU ALL RIGHT?
YEAH, I GUESS SO, FATHER. IT WAS A CLOSE THING, THOUGH...
THEN LAND AND CONTACT THUNDERBIRD TWO. VIRGIL AND BRAINS ARE ON THEIR WAY!
AN HOUR LATER...
FRANK BELLAMY
OH, BOY, AM I GLAD TO SEE YOU TWO! THINGS ARE HOTTING UP!
THESE THINGS TURNED INTO STONE, SCOTT... I'D LIKE TO SEE THEM.
THE LITTLE SCIENTIST WORKS FAST...
HMM... I CAN'T SAY TOO MUCH WITHOUT A PROPER LABORATORY EXAMINATION, BUT IT LOOKS AS THOUGH THIS CREATURE IS CAPABLE OF CAUSING INSTANT FOSSILIZATION.
WHAT'S THE NEXT MOVE, BRAINS?
WE BROUGHT THE MOLE WITH US. I'D LIKE TO FOLLOW THE BEAST AND HAVE A CLOSER LOOK.
THEN TAKE VIRGIL WITH YOU - AND FOR GOODNESS' SAKE BE CAREFUL!
THE BURROWING MACHINE TRUNDLES OFF...

Artist: Frank Bellamy

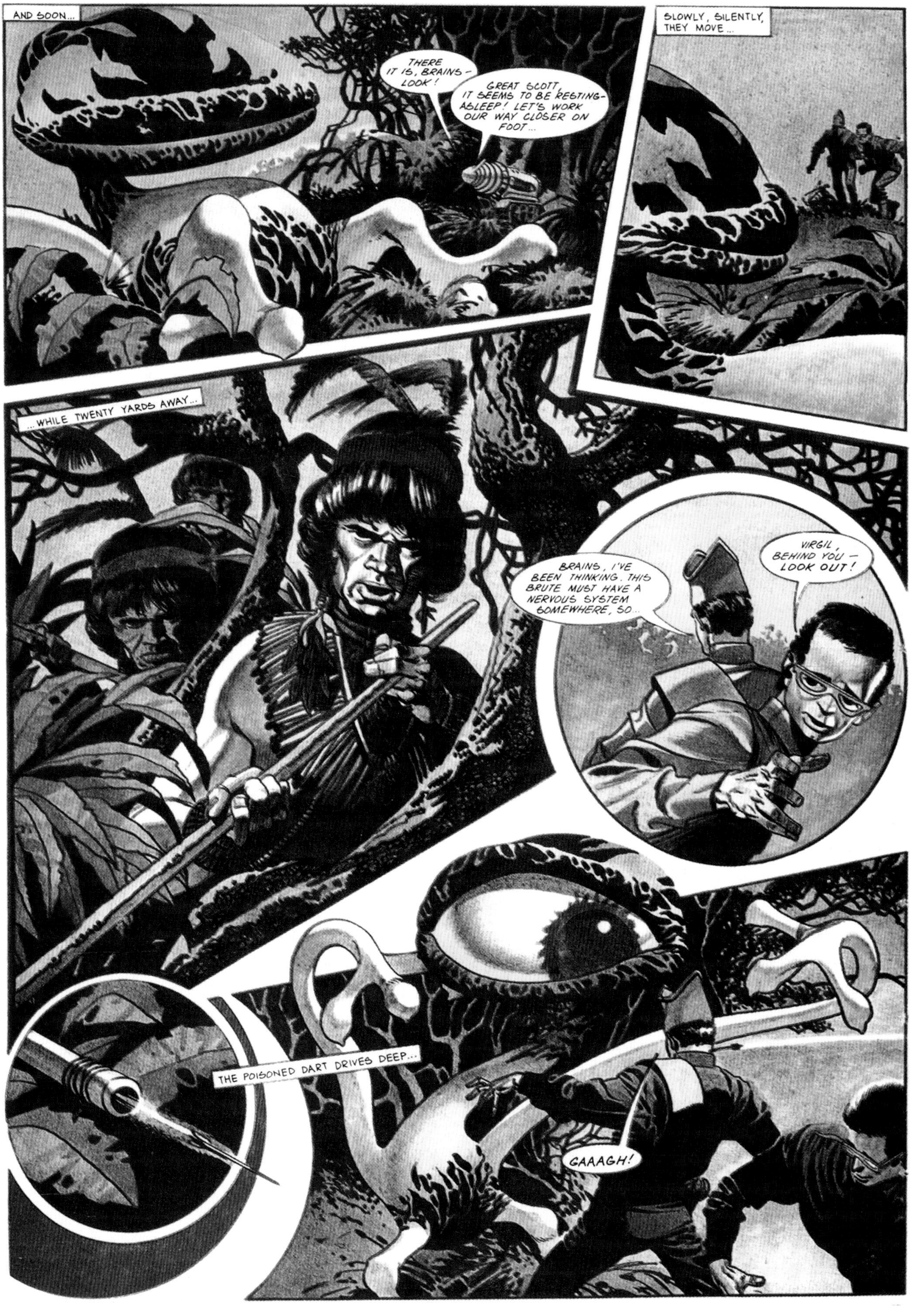
AND SOON...
THERE IT IS, BRAINS - LOOK!
GREAT SCOTT, IT SEEMS TO BE RESTING-ASLEEP! LET'S WORK OUR WAY CLOSER ON FOOT...
SLOWLY, SILENTLY, THEY MOVE...
...WHILE TWENTY YARDS AWAY...
BRAINS, I'VE BEEN THINKING. THIS BRUTE MUST HAVE A NERVOUS SYSTEM SOMEWHERE, SO...
VIRGIL, BEHIND YOU - LOOK OUT!
THE POISONED DART DRIVES DEEP...
GAAAGH!

Part 6 - dateline 16 December 2067

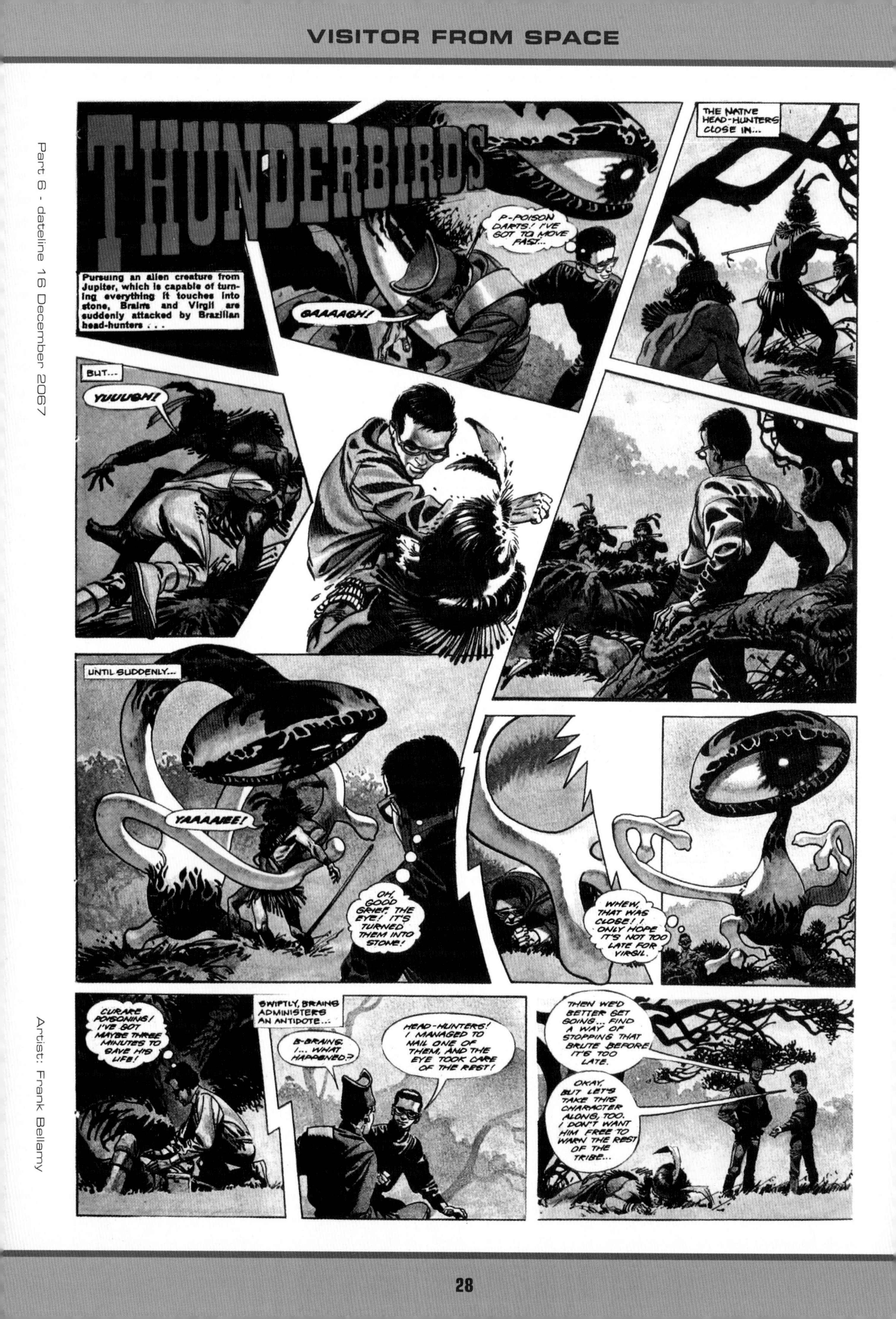
THUNDERBIRDS
Pursuing an alien creature from Jupiter, which is capable of turning everything it touches into stone, Brains and Virgil are suddenly attacked by Brazilian head-hunters . . .
P-POISON DARTS! I'VE GOT TO MOVE FAST...
GAAAAGH!
THE NATIVE HEAD-HUNTERS CLOSE IN...
BUT...
YUUUGH!
UNTIL SUDDENLY...
YAAAAIEE!
OH, GOOD GRIEF, THE EYE! IT'S TURNED THEM INTO STONE!
WHEW, THAT WAS CLOSE! I ONLY HOPE IT'S NOT TOO LATE FOR VIRGIL.
CURARE POISONING! I'VE GOT MAYBE THREE MINUTES TO SAVE HIS LIFE!
SWIFTLY, BRAINS ADMINISTERS AN ANTIDOTE...
B-BRAINS. I... WHAT HAPPENED?
HEAD-HUNTERS! I MANAGED TO NAIL ONE OF THEM, AND THE EYE TOOK CARE OF THE REST!
THEN WE'D BETTER GET GOING... FIND A WAY OF STOPPING THAT BRUTE BEFORE IT'S TOO LATE.
OKAY, BUT LET'S TAKE THIS CHARACTER ALONG, TOO. I DON'T WANT HIM FREE TO WARN THE REST OF THE TRIBE...

Artist: Frank Bellamy

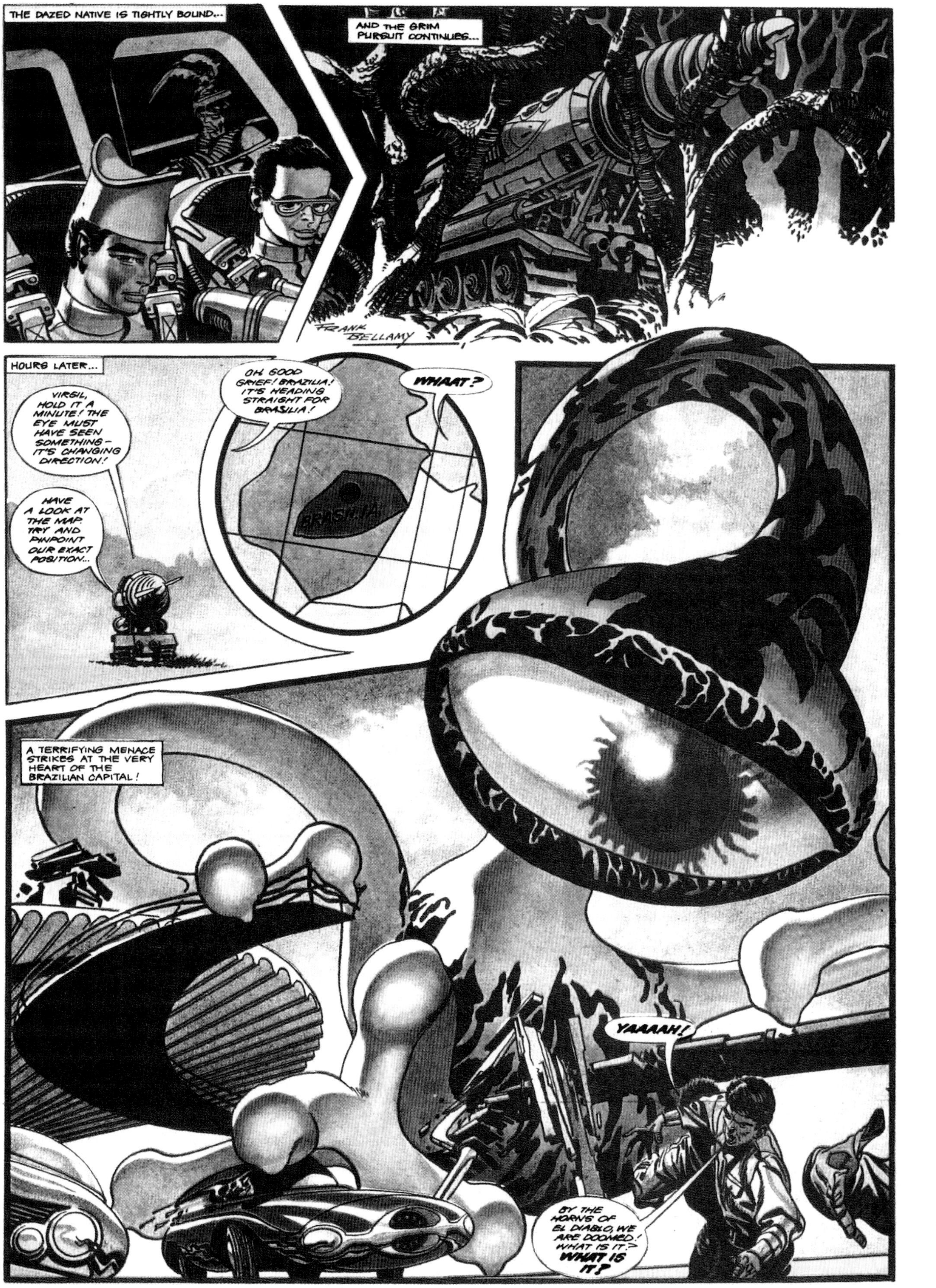
THE DAZED NATIVE IS TIGHTLY BOUND...
AND THE GRIM PURSUIT CONTINUES...
FRANK BELLAMY
HOURS LATER...
VIRGIL, HOLD IT A MINUTE! THE EYE MUST HAVE SEEN SOMETHING – IT'S CHANGING DIRECTION!
HAVE A LOOK AT THE MAP. TRY AND PINPOINT OUR EXACT POSITION...
OH, GOOD GRIEF! BRAZILIA! IT'S HEADING STRAIGHT FOR BRASILIA!
WHAAT?
BRASILIA
A TERRIFYING MENACE STRIKES AT THE VERY HEART OF THE BRAZILIAN CAPITAL!
YAAAAH!
BY THE HORNS OF EL DIABLO, WE ARE DOOMED! WHAT IS IT? WHAT IS IT?

Part 7 - dateline 23 December 2067

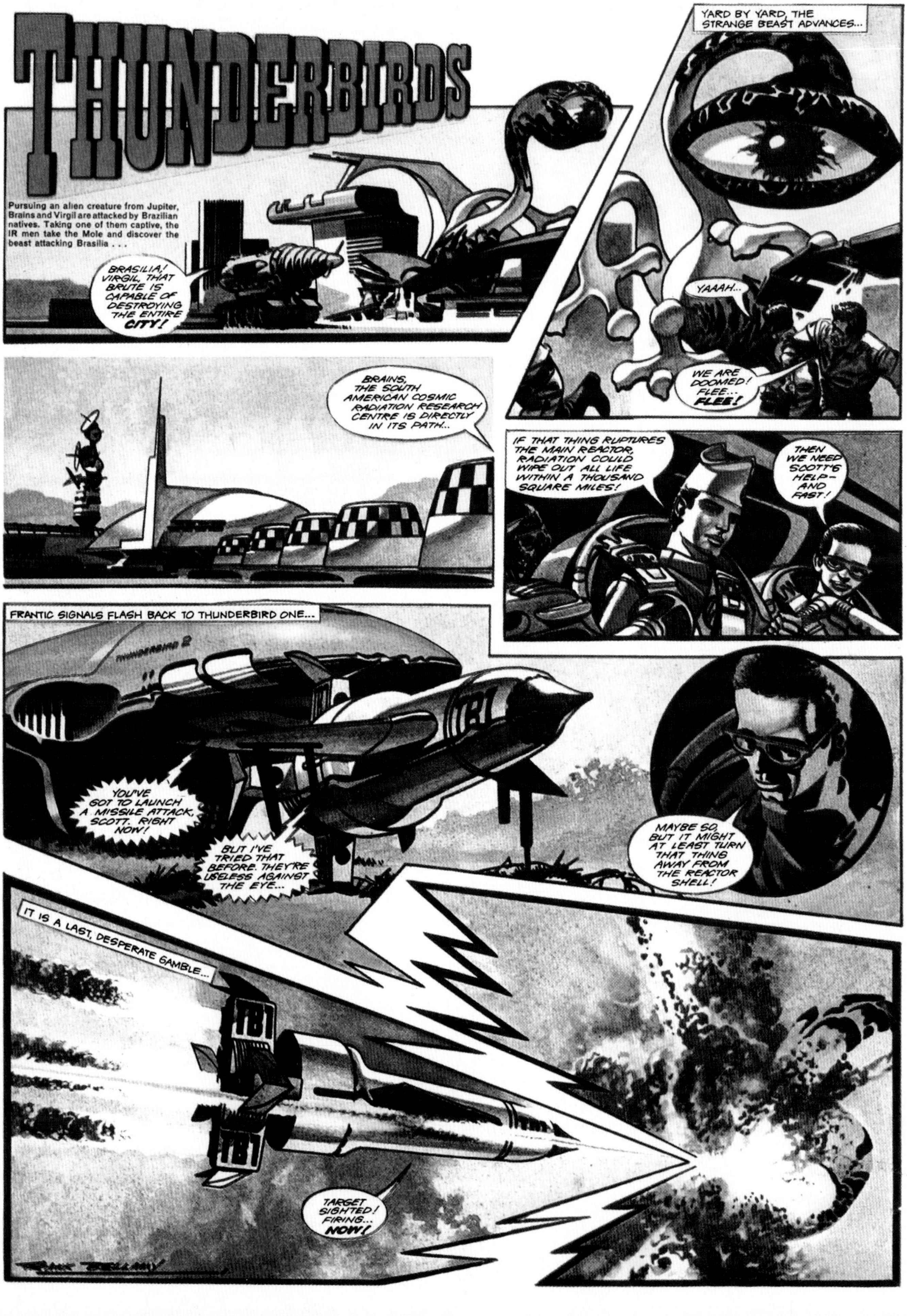
THUNDERBIRDS
Pursuing an alien creature from Jupiter, Brains and Virgil are attacked by Brazilian natives. Taking one of them captive, the IR men take the Mole and discover the beast attacking Brasilia . . .
BRASILIA! VIRGIL, THAT BRUTE IS CAPABLE OF DESTROYING THE ENTIRE CITY!
YARD BY YARD, THE STRANGE BEAST ADVANCES...
YAAAH...
WE ARE DOOMED! FLEE... FLEE!
BRAINS, THE SOUTH AMERICAN COSMIC RADIATION RESEARCH CENTRE IS DIRECTLY IN ITS PATH...
IF THAT THING RUPTURES THE MAIN REACTOR, RADIATION COULD WIPE OUT ALL LIFE WITHIN A THOUSAND SQUARE MILES!
THEN WE NEED SCOTT'S HELP— AND FAST!
FRANTIC SIGNALS FLASH BACK TO THUNDERBIRD ONE...
YOU'VE GOT TO LAUNCH A MISSILE ATTACK, SCOTT. RIGHT NOW!
BUT I'VE TRIED THAT BEFORE. THEY'RE USELESS AGAINST THE EYE...
MAYBE SO, BUT IT MIGHT AT LEAST TURN THAT THING AWAY FROM THE REACTOR SHELL!
IT IS A LAST, DESPERATE GAMBLE...
TARGET SIGHTED! FIRING... NOW!
FRANK BELLAMY

Artist: Frank Bellamy

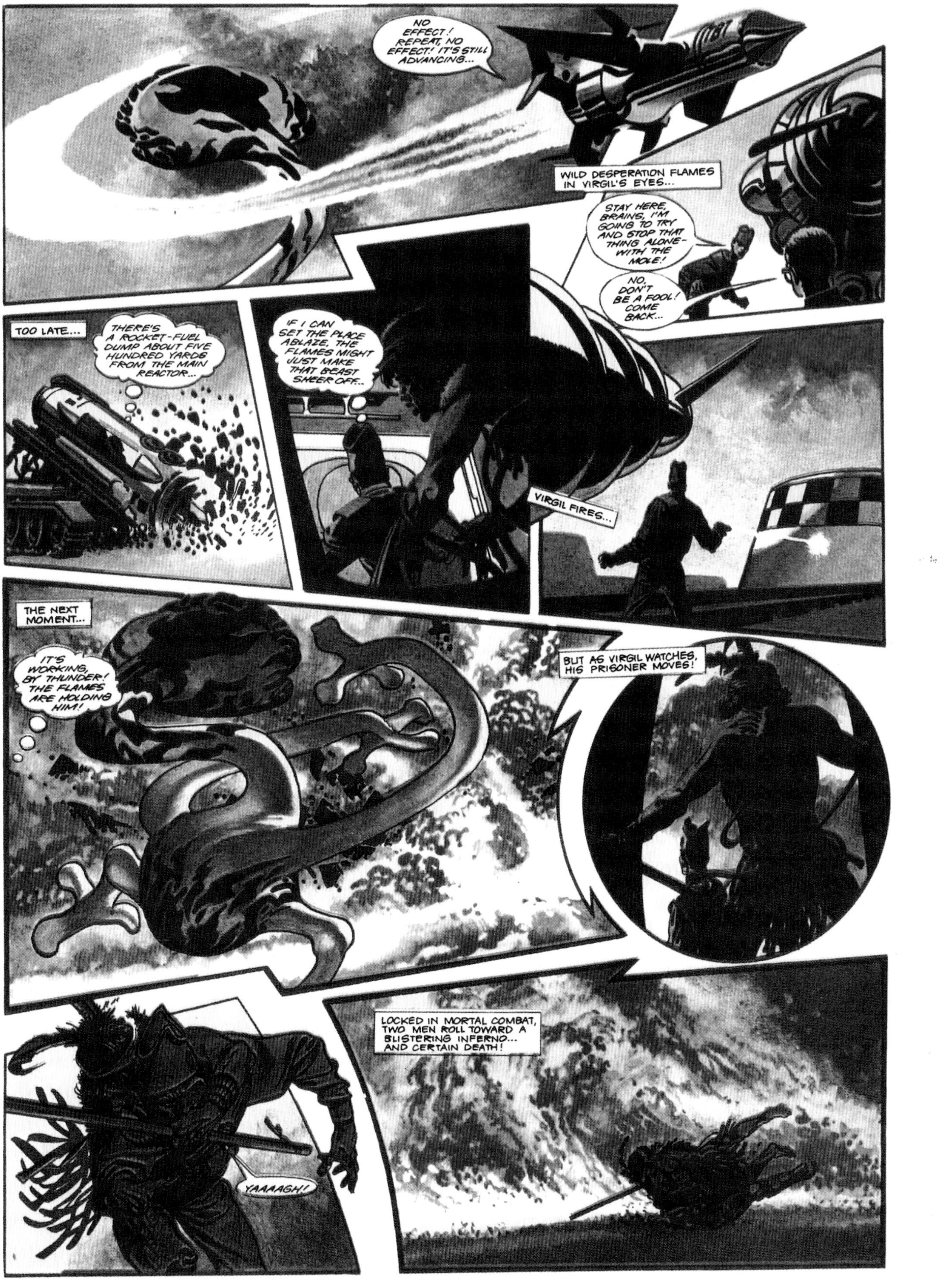
NO EFFECT! REPEAT, NO EFFECT! IT'S STILL ADVANCING...
WILD DESPERATION FLAMES IN VIRGIL'S EYES...
STAY HERE, BRAINS, I'M GOING TO TRY AND STOP THAT THING ALONE - WITH THE MOLE!
NO, DON'T BE A FOOL! COME BACK...
TOO LATE...
THERE'S A ROCKET-FUEL DUMP ABOUT FIVE HUNDRED YARDS FROM THE MAIN REACTOR...
IF I CAN SET THE PLACE ABLAZE, THE FLAMES MIGHT JUST MAKE THAT BEAST SHEER OFF...
VIRGIL FIRES...
THE NEXT MOMENT...
IT'S WORKING, BY THUNDER! THE FLAMES ARE HOLDING HIM!
BUT AS VIRGIL WATCHES, HIS PRISONER MOVES!
YAAAAGH!
LOCKED IN MORTAL COMBAT, TWO MEN ROLL TOWARD A BLISTERING INFERNO... AND CERTAIN DEATH!

Part 8 - dateline 30 December 2067

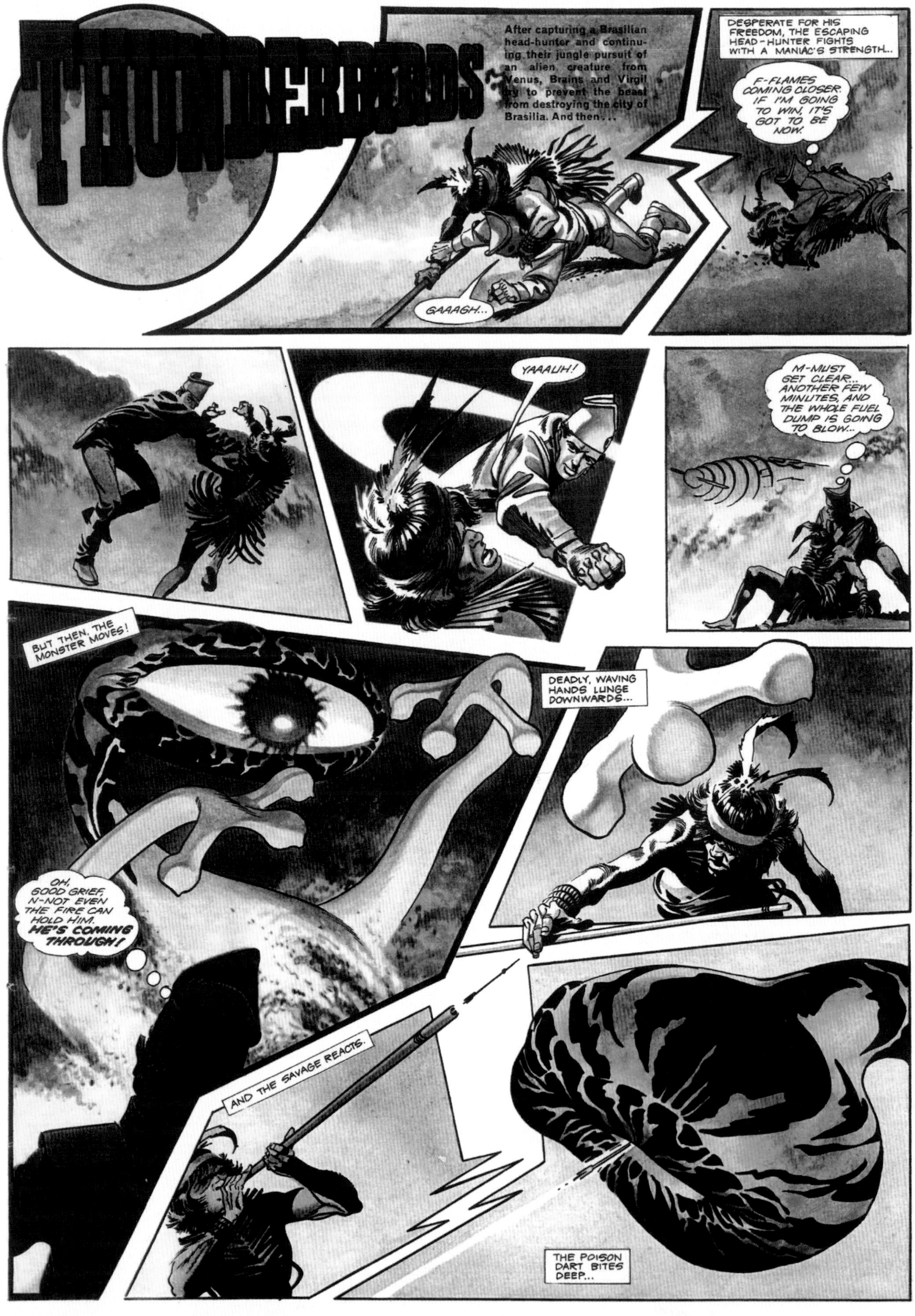
THUNDERBIRDS
After capturing a Brasilian head-hunter and continuing their jungle pursuit of an alien creature from Venus, Brains and Virgil try to prevent the beast from destroying the city of Brasilia. And then...
GAAAGH...
DESPERATE FOR HIS FREEDOM, THE ESCAPING HEAD-HUNTER FIGHTS WITH A MANIAC'S STRENGTH...
F-FLAMES COMING CLOSER. IF I'M GOING TO WIN, IT'S GOT TO BE NOW.
YAAAUH!
M-MUST GET CLEAR... ANOTHER FEW MINUTES, AND THE WHOLE FUEL DUMP IS GOING TO BLOW...
BUT THEN, THE MONSTER MOVES!
OH, GOOD GRIEF. N-NOT EVEN THE FIRE CAN HOLD HIM. HE'S COMING THROUGH!
DEADLY, WAVING HANDS LUNGE DOWNWARDS...
AND THE SAVAGE REACTS.
THE POISON DART BITES DEEP...

Artist: Frank Bellamy

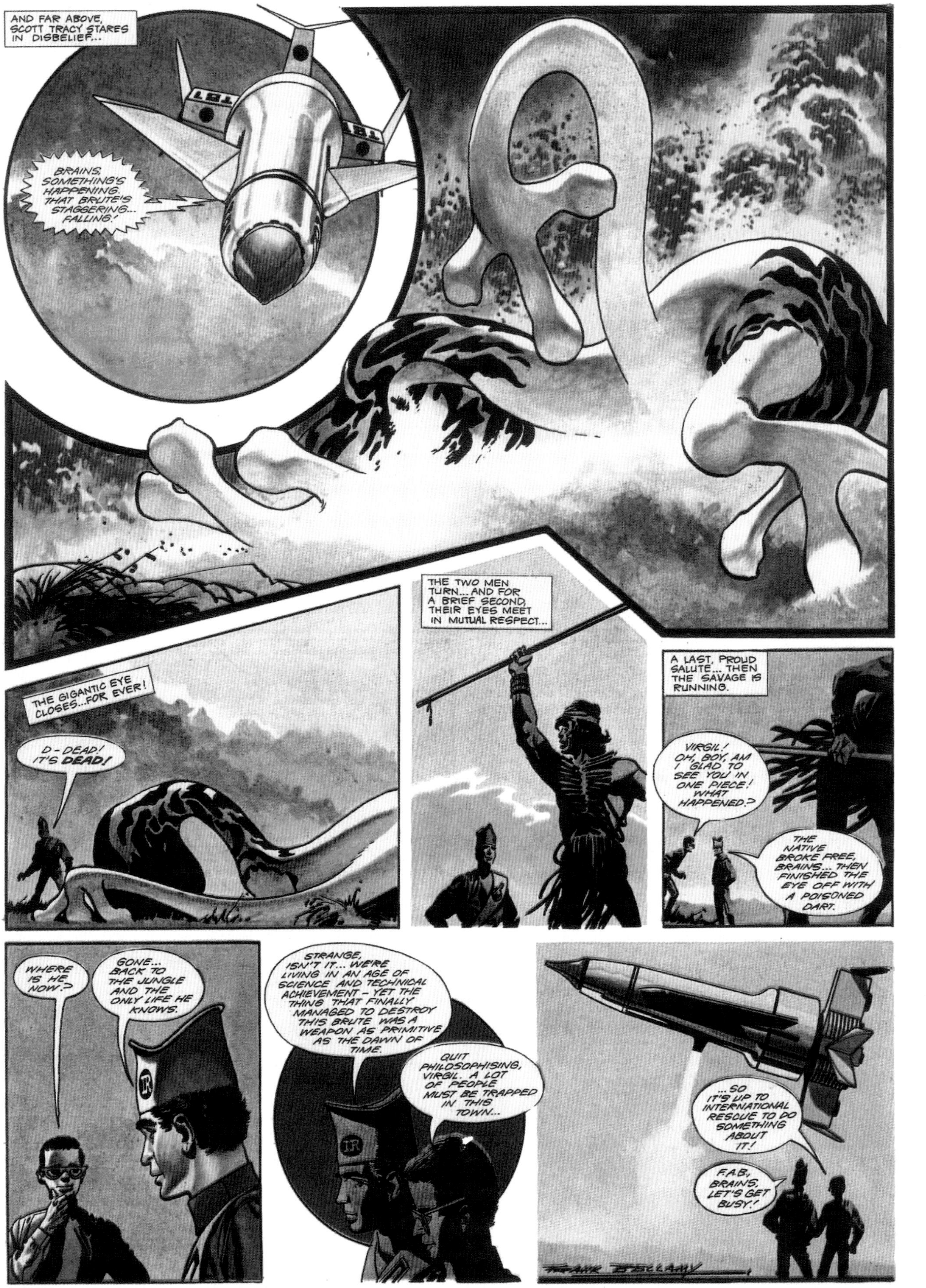
AND FAR ABOVE, SCOTT TRACY STARES IN DISBELIEF...
BRAINS, SOMETHING'S HAPPENING. THAT BRUTE'S STAGGERING... FALLING!
THE TWO MEN TURN... AND FOR A BRIEF SECOND, THEIR EYES MEET IN MUTUAL RESPECT...
A LAST, PROUD SALUTE... THEN THE SAVAGE IS RUNNING.
THE GIGANTIC EYE CLOSES...FOR EVER!
D-DEAD! IT'S DEAD!
VIRGIL! OH, BOY, AM I GLAD TO SEE YOU IN ONE PIECE! WHAT HAPPENED?
THE NATIVE BROKE FREE, BRAINS... THEN FINISHED THE EYE OFF WITH A POISONED DART.
WHERE IS HE NOW?
GONE... BACK TO THE JUNGLE AND THE ONLY LIFE HE KNOWS.
STRANGE, ISN'T IT... WE'RE LIVING IN AN AGE OF SCIENCE AND TECHNICAL ACHIEVEMENT - YET THE THING THAT FINALLY MANAGED TO DESTROY THIS BRUTE WAS A WEAPON AS PRIMITIVE AS THE DAWN OF TIME.
QUIT PHILOSOPHISING, VIRGIL. A LOT OF PEOPLE MUST BE TRAPPED IN THIS TOWN...
...SO IT'S UP TO INTERNATIONAL RESCUE TO DO SOMETHING ABOUT IT!
F.A.B., BRAINS, LET'S GET BUSY!
FRANK BELLAMY

Part 1 - dateline 06 January 2068

THUNDERBIRDS

Artist: Frank Bellamy

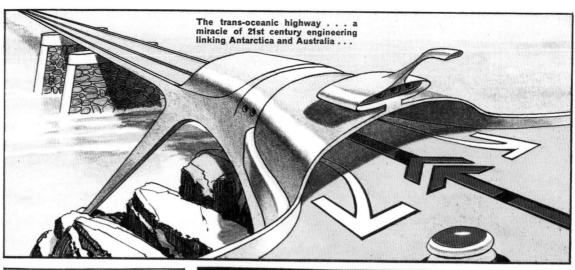

The trans-oceanic highway . . . a miracle of 21st century engineering linking Antarctica and Australia . . .

AN EXCITED VIDEO-SCAN COMMENTATOR DESCRIBES THE OPENING CEREMONY...

THE TAPE BREAKS, AND NOW THE FIRST CONVOY OF HOVER-TRUCKS IS ON ITS WAY...

SOON, VAST QUANTITIES OF MINERALS AND RAW MATERIALS WILL BE FLOWING NORTHWARDS FROM THIS ICE-BOUND CONTINENT TO AUSTRALIA'S HUNGRY REFINING PLANTS...

BUT TWO MILES AWAY, ANOTHER, STRANGER SCENE IS UNFOLDING...

CONTROL TO PENGUIN STRIKE UNIT. CLOSE IN!

ADVANCE IN OPEN ORDER. FIRE AT WILL!

A GLISTENING SPRAY OF OIL GLOBULES FANS ACROSS THE ROAD...

AND FIFTEEN MINUTES LATER...

JOE, LOOK OUT! SHE'S SLIDING!

JACK-KNIFE! I-I CAN'T HOLD HER!

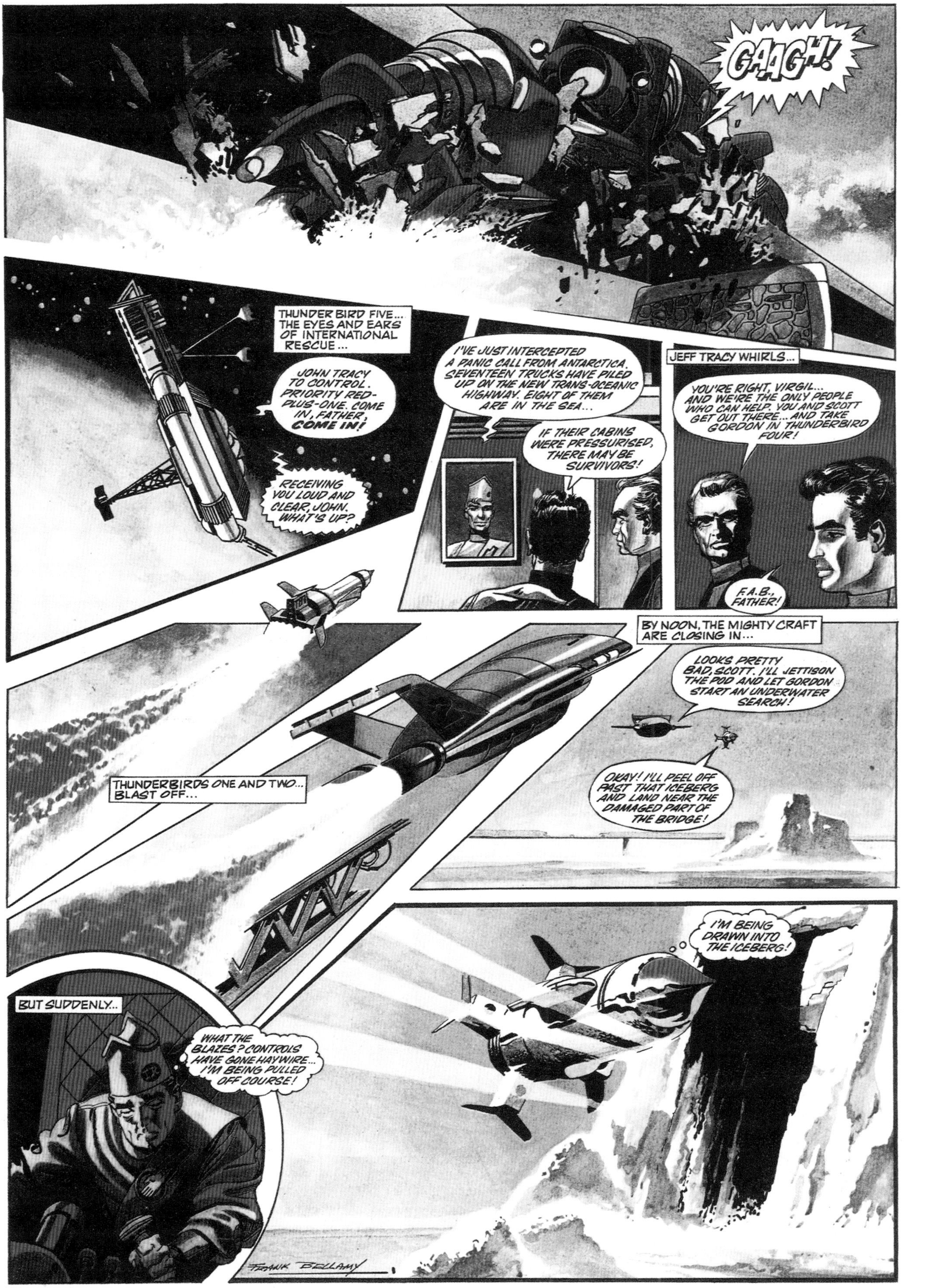
GAAGH!
THUNDER BIRD FIVE... THE EYES AND EARS OF INTERNATIONAL RESCUE...
JOHN TRACY TO CONTROL. PRIORITY RED-PLUS-ONE. COME IN, FATHER, COME IN!
RECEIVING YOU LOUD AND CLEAR, JOHN. WHAT'S UP?
I'VE JUST INTERCEPTED A PANIC CALL FROM ANTARCTICA. SEVENTEEN TRUCKS HAVE PILED UP ON THE NEW TRANS-OCEANIC HIGHWAY. EIGHT OF THEM ARE IN THE SEA...
IF THEIR CABINS WERE PRESSURISED, THERE MAY BE SURVIVORS!
JEFF TRACY WHIRLS...
YOU'RE RIGHT, VIRGIL... AND WE'RE THE ONLY PEOPLE WHO CAN HELP. YOU AND SCOTT GET OUT THERE... AND TAKE GORDON IN THUNDERBIRD FOUR!
F.A.B., FATHER!
THUNDERBIRDS ONE AND TWO... BLAST OFF...
BY NOON, THE MIGHTY CRAFT ARE CLOSING IN...
LOOKS PRETTY BAD, SCOTT. I'LL JETTISON THE POD AND LET GORDON START AN UNDERWATER SEARCH!
OKAY! I'LL PEEL OFF PAST THAT ICEBERG AND LAND NEAR THE DAMAGED PART OF THE BRIDGE!
BUT SUDDENLY...
WHAT THE BLAZES? CONTROLS HAVE GONE HAYWIRE... I'M BEING PULLED OFF COURSE!
I'M BEING DRAWN INTO THE ICEBERG!
FRANK BELLAMY

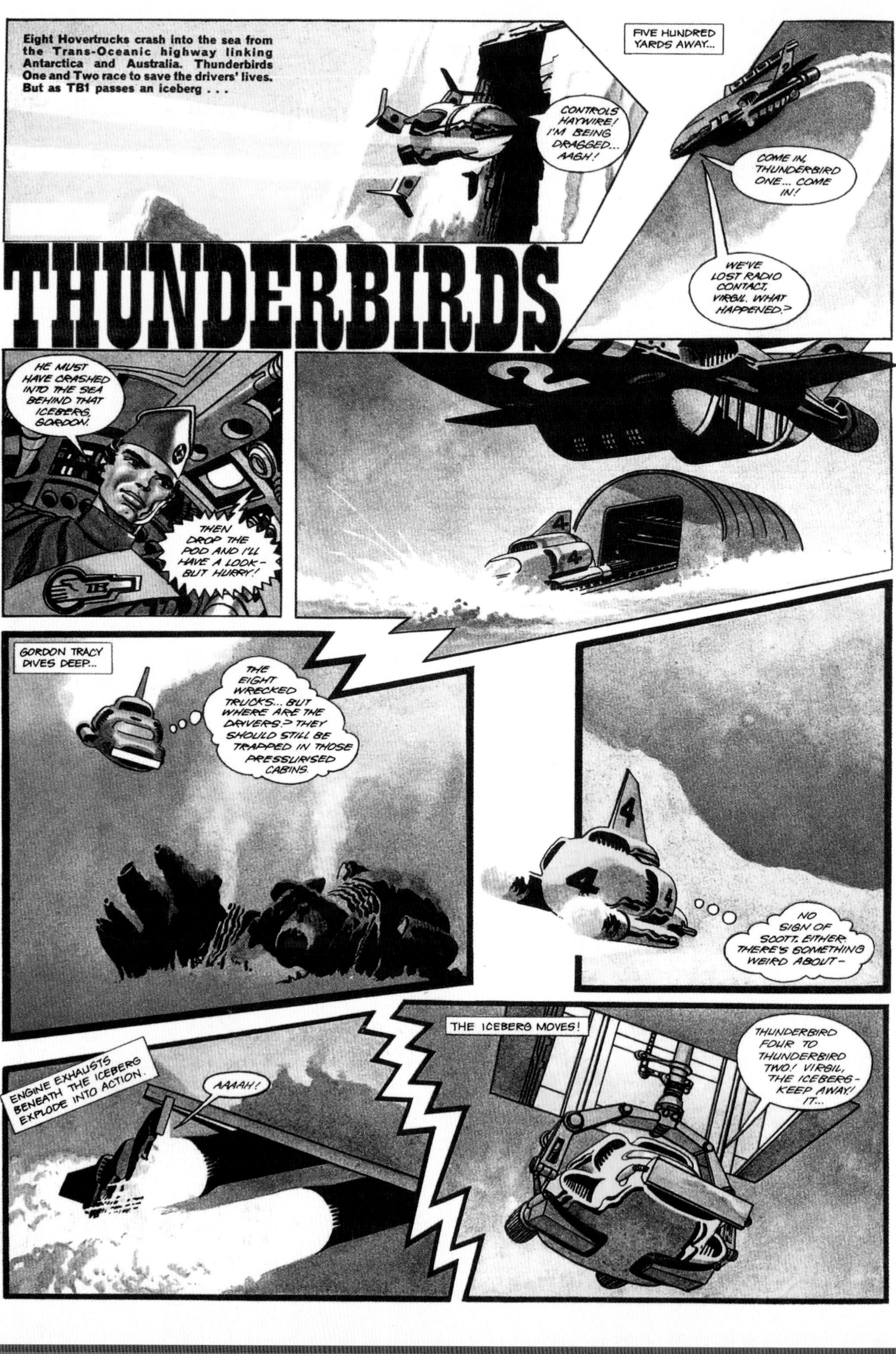
Eight Hovertrucks crash into the sea from the Trans-Oceanic highway linking Antarctica and Australia. Thunderbirds One and Two race to save the drivers' lives. But as TB1 passes an iceberg . . .
CONTROLS HAYWIRE! I'M BEING DRAGGED... AAGH!
FIVE HUNDRED YARDS AWAY...
COME IN, THUNDERBIRD ONE... COME IN!
THUNDERBIRDS
WE'VE LOST RADIO CONTACT, VIRGIL. WHAT HAPPENED?
HE MUST HAVE CRASHED INTO THE SEA BEHIND THAT ICEBERG, GORDON.
THEN DROP THE POD AND I'LL HAVE A LOOK - BUT HURRY!
GORDON TRACY DIVES DEEP...
THE EIGHT WRECKED TRUCKS... BUT WHERE ARE THE DRIVERS? THEY SHOULD STILL BE TRAPPED IN THOSE PRESSURISED CABINS.
NO SIGN OF SCOTT, EITHER. THERE'S SOMETHING WEIRD ABOUT -
ENGINE EXHAUSTS BENEATH THE ICEBERG EXPLODE INTO ACTION.
AAAAH!
THE ICEBERG MOVES!
THUNDERBIRD FOUR TO THUNDERBIRD TWO! VIRGIL, THE ICEBERG - KEEP AWAY! IT...

Artist: Frank Bellamy

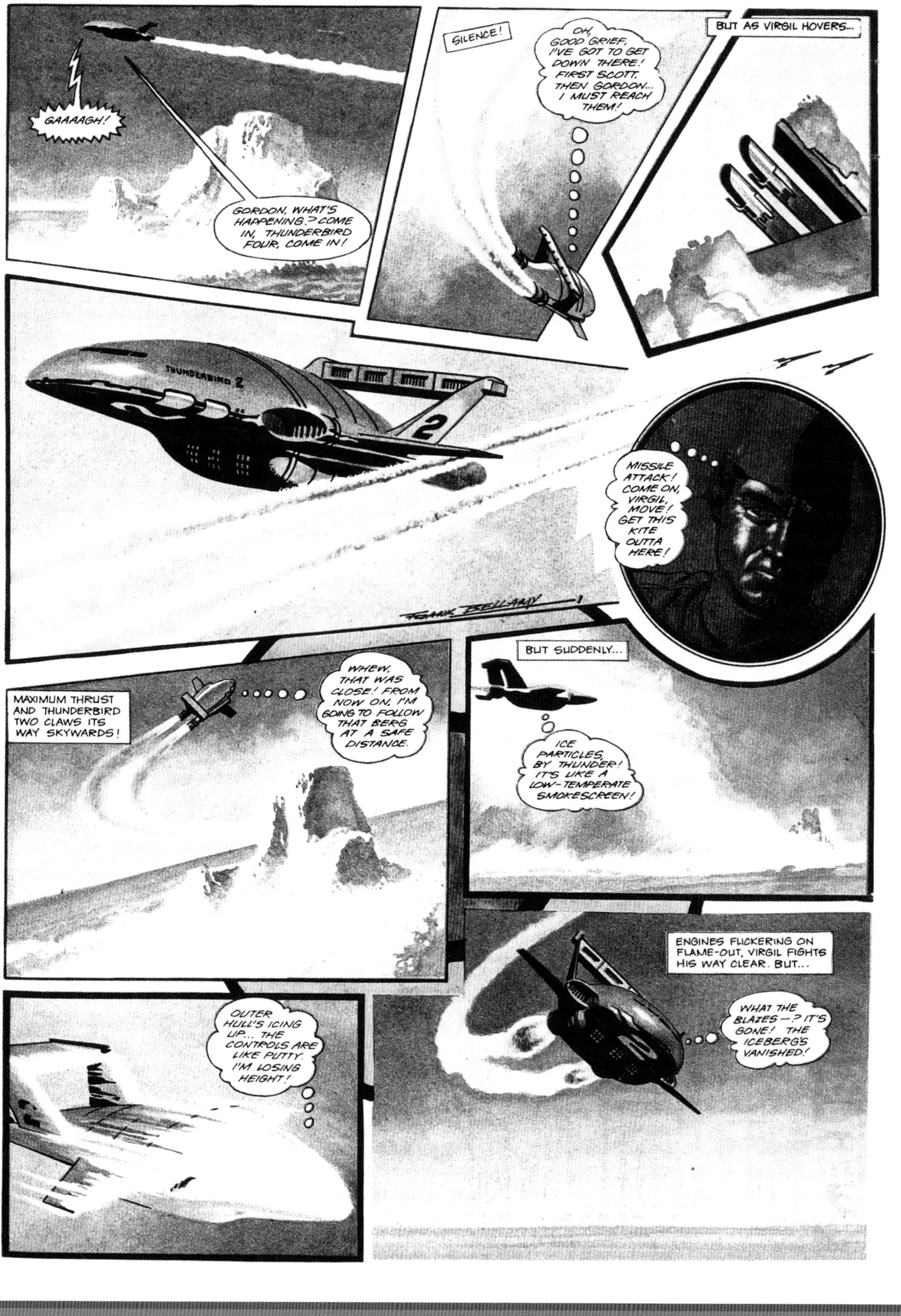
GAAAAGH!
GORDON, WHAT'S HAPPENING? COME IN, THUNDERBIRD FOUR, COME IN!
SILENCE!
OH, GOOD GRIEF, I'VE GOT TO GET DOWN THERE! FIRST SCOTT, THEN GORDON... I MUST REACH THEM!
BUT AS VIRGIL HOVERS...
THUNDERBIRD 2
MISSILE ATTACK! COME ON, VIRGIL, MOVE! GET THIS KITE OUTTA HERE!
FRANK BELLAMY
MAXIMUM THRUST AND THUNDERBIRD TWO CLAWS ITS WAY SKYWARDS!
WHEW, THAT WAS CLOSE! FROM NOW ON, I'M GOING TO FOLLOW THAT BERG AT A SAFE DISTANCE.
BUT SUDDENLY...
ICE PARTICLES, BY THUNDER! IT'S LIKE A LOW-TEMPERATE SMOKESCREEN!
OUTER HULL'S ICING UP... THE CONTROLS ARE LIKE PUTTY. I'M LOSING HEIGHT!
ENGINES FLICKERING ON FLAME-OUT, VIRGIL FIGHTS HIS WAY CLEAR. BUT...
WHAT THE BLAZES—? IT'S GONE! THE ICEBERG'S VANISHED!

Part 3 - dateline 20 January 2068

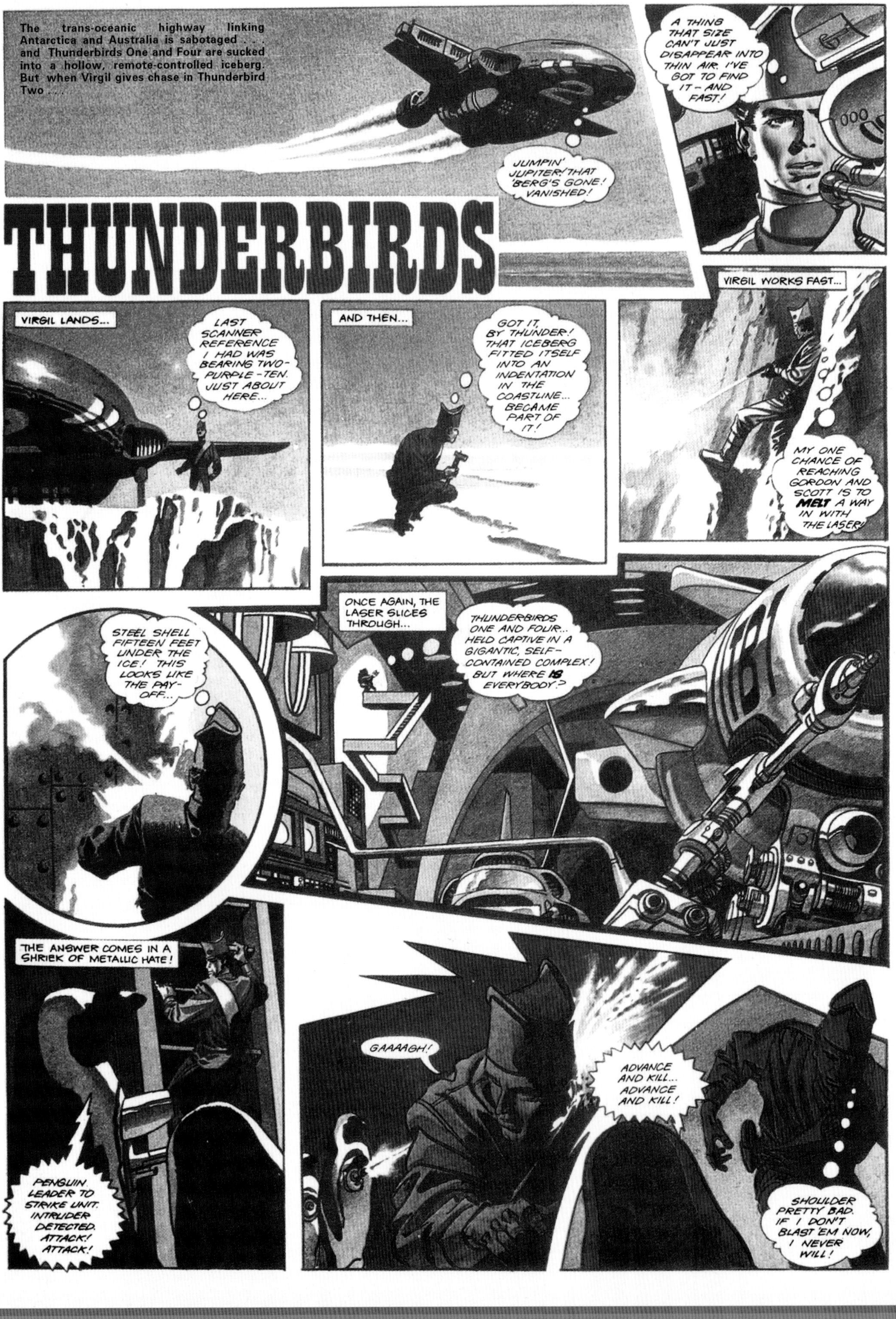
The trans-oceanic highway linking Antarctica and Australia is sabotaged . . . and Thunderbirds One and Four are sucked into a hollow, remote-controlled iceberg. But when Virgil gives chase in Thunderbird Two . . .
JUMPIN' JUPITER! THAT 'BERG'S GONE! VANISHED!
A THING THAT SIZE CAN'T JUST DISAPPEAR INTO THIN AIR. I'VE GOT TO FIND IT - AND FAST!
THUNDERBIRDS
VIRGIL LANDS...
LAST SCANNER REFERENCE I HAD WAS BEARING TWO-PURPLE-TEN. JUST ABOUT HERE...
AND THEN...
GOT IT, BY THUNDER! THAT ICEBERG FITTED ITSELF INTO AN INDENTATION IN THE COASTLINE... BECAME PART OF IT!
VIRGIL WORKS FAST...
MY ONE CHANCE OF REACHING GORDON AND SCOTT IS TO MELT A WAY IN WITH THE LASER!
STEEL SHELL FIFTEEN FEET UNDER THE ICE! THIS LOOKS LIKE THE PAY-OFF...
ONCE AGAIN, THE LASER SLICES THROUGH...
THUNDERBIRDS ONE AND FOUR... HELD CAPTIVE IN A GIGANTIC, SELF-CONTAINED COMPLEX! BUT WHERE IS EVERYBODY?
THE ANSWER COMES IN A SHRIEK OF METALLIC HATE!
PENGUIN LEADER TO STRIKE UNIT. INTRUDER DETECTED. ATTACK! ATTACK!
GAAAAGH!
ADVANCE AND KILL... ADVANCE AND KILL!
SHOULDER PRETTY BAD. IF I DON'T BLAST 'EM NOW, I NEVER WILL!

Artist: Frank Bellamy

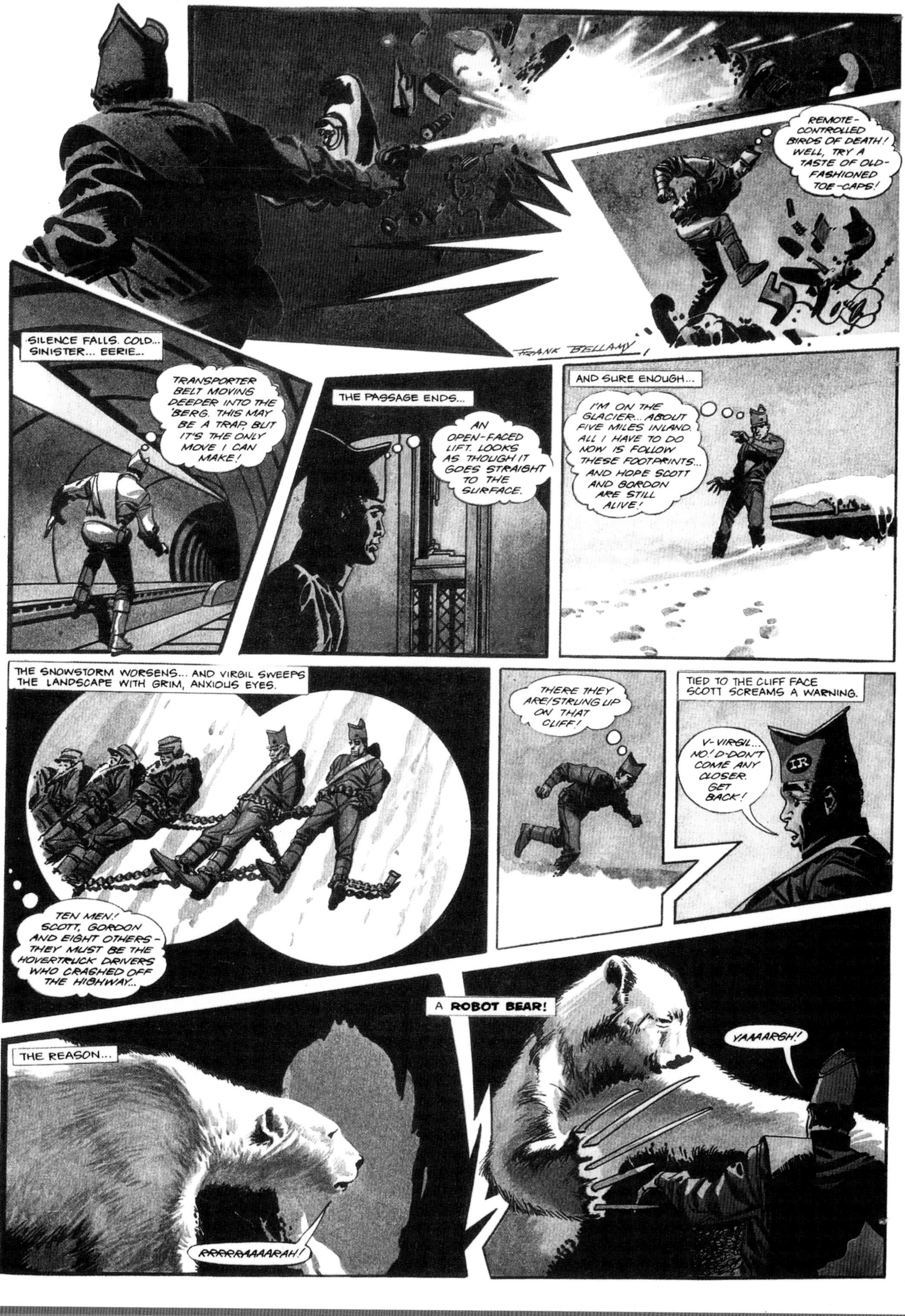
REMOTE-CONTROLLED BIRDS OF DEATH! WELL, TRY A TASTE OF OLD-FASHIONED TOE-CAPS!
FRANK BELLAMY
SILENCE FALLS. COLD... SINISTER... EERIE...
TRANSPORTER BELT MOVING DEEPER INTO THE 'BERG. THIS MAY BE A TRAP, BUT IT'S THE ONLY MOVE I CAN MAKE!
THE PASSAGE ENDS...
AN OPEN-FACED LIFT. LOOKS AS THOUGH IT GOES STRAIGHT TO THE SURFACE.
AND SURE ENOUGH...
I'M ON THE GLACIER... ABOUT FIVE MILES INLAND. ALL I HAVE TO DO NOW IS FOLLOW THESE FOOTPRINTS... AND HOPE SCOTT AND GORDON ARE STILL ALIVE!
THE SNOWSTORM WORSENS... AND VIRGIL SWEEPS THE LANDSCAPE WITH GRIM, ANXIOUS EYES.
TEN MEN! SCOTT, GORDON AND EIGHT OTHERS - THEY MUST BE THE HOVERTRUCK DRIVERS WHO CRASHED OFF THE HIGHWAY...
THERE THEY ARE! STRUNG UP ON THAT CLIFF!
TIED TO THE CLIFF FACE SCOTT SCREAMS A WARNING.
V-VIRGIL... NO! D-DON'T COME ANY CLOSER. GET BACK!
IR
THE REASON...
RRRRRAAAARAH!
A ROBOT BEAR!
YAAAARGH!

Part 4 - dateline 27 January 2068

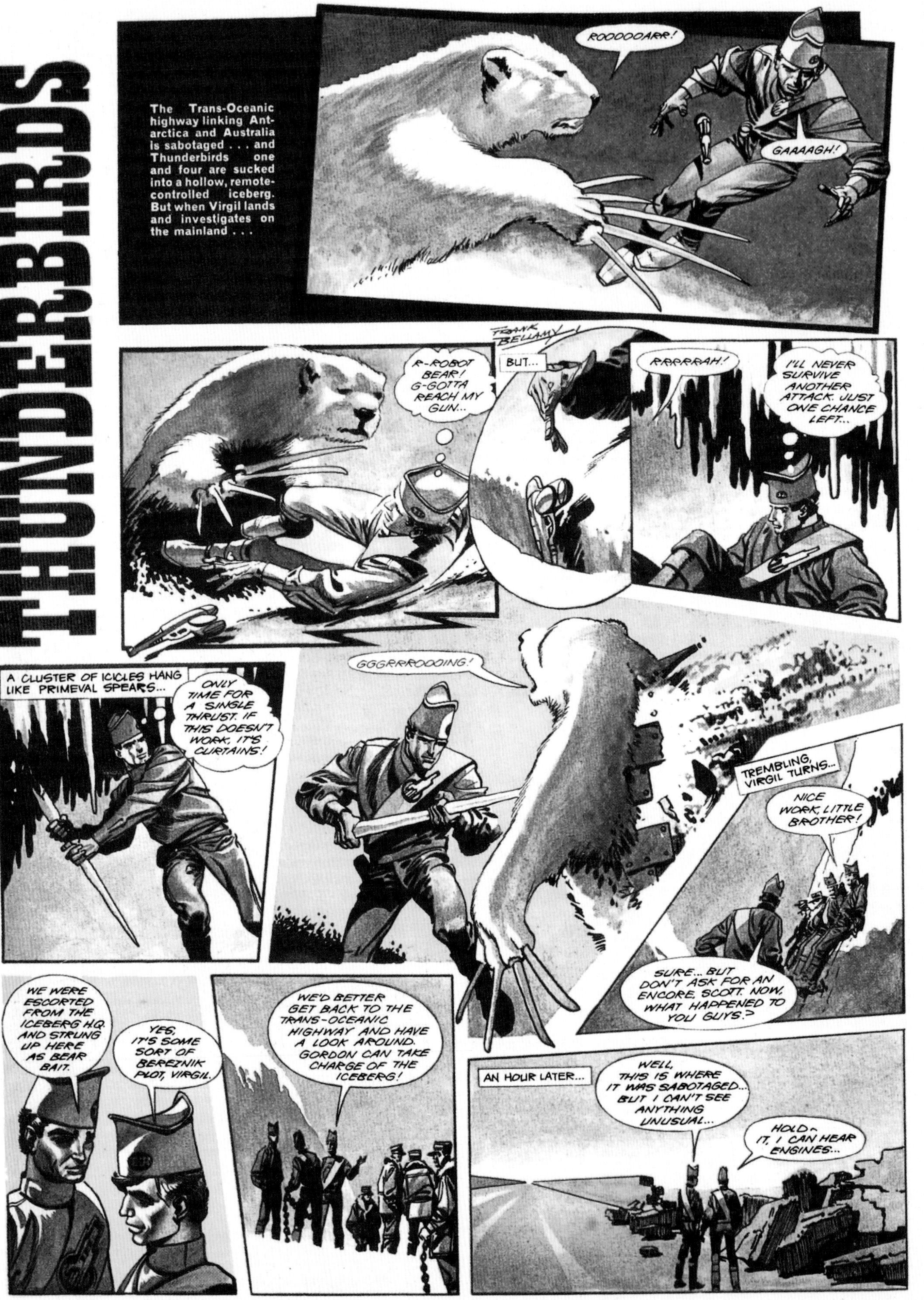
THUNDERBIRDS
The Trans-Oceanic highway linking Antarctica and Australia is sabotaged . . . and Thunderbirds one and four are sucked into a hollow, remote-controlled iceberg. But when Virgil lands and investigates on the mainland . . .
ROOOOOARR!
GAAAAGH!
FRANK BELLAMY
R-ROBOT BEAR! G-GOTTA REACH MY GUN...
BUT...
RRRRRAH!
I'LL NEVER SURVIVE ANOTHER ATTACK. JUST ONE CHANCE LEFT...
A CLUSTER OF ICICLES HANG LIKE PRIMEVAL SPEARS...
ONLY TIME FOR A SINGLE THRUST. IF THIS DOESN'T WORK, IT'S CURTAINS!
GGGRRROOOING!
TREMBLING, VIRGIL TURNS...
NICE WORK, LITTLE BROTHER!
SURE... BUT DON'T ASK FOR AN ENCORE, SCOTT. NOW, WHAT HAPPENED TO YOU GUYS?
WE WERE ESCORTED FROM THE ICEBERG H.Q. AND STRUNG UP HERE AS BEAR BAIT.
YES, IT'S SOME SORT OF BEREZNIK PLOT, VIRGIL.
WE'D BETTER GET BACK TO THE TRANS-OCEANIC HIGHWAY AND HAVE A LOOK AROUND. GORDON CAN TAKE CHARGE OF THE ICEBERG!
AN HOUR LATER...
WELL, THIS IS WHERE IT WAS SABOTAGED... BUT I CAN'T SEE ANYTHING UNUSUAL...
HOLD - IT, I CAN HEAR ENGINES...

Artist: Frank Bellamy

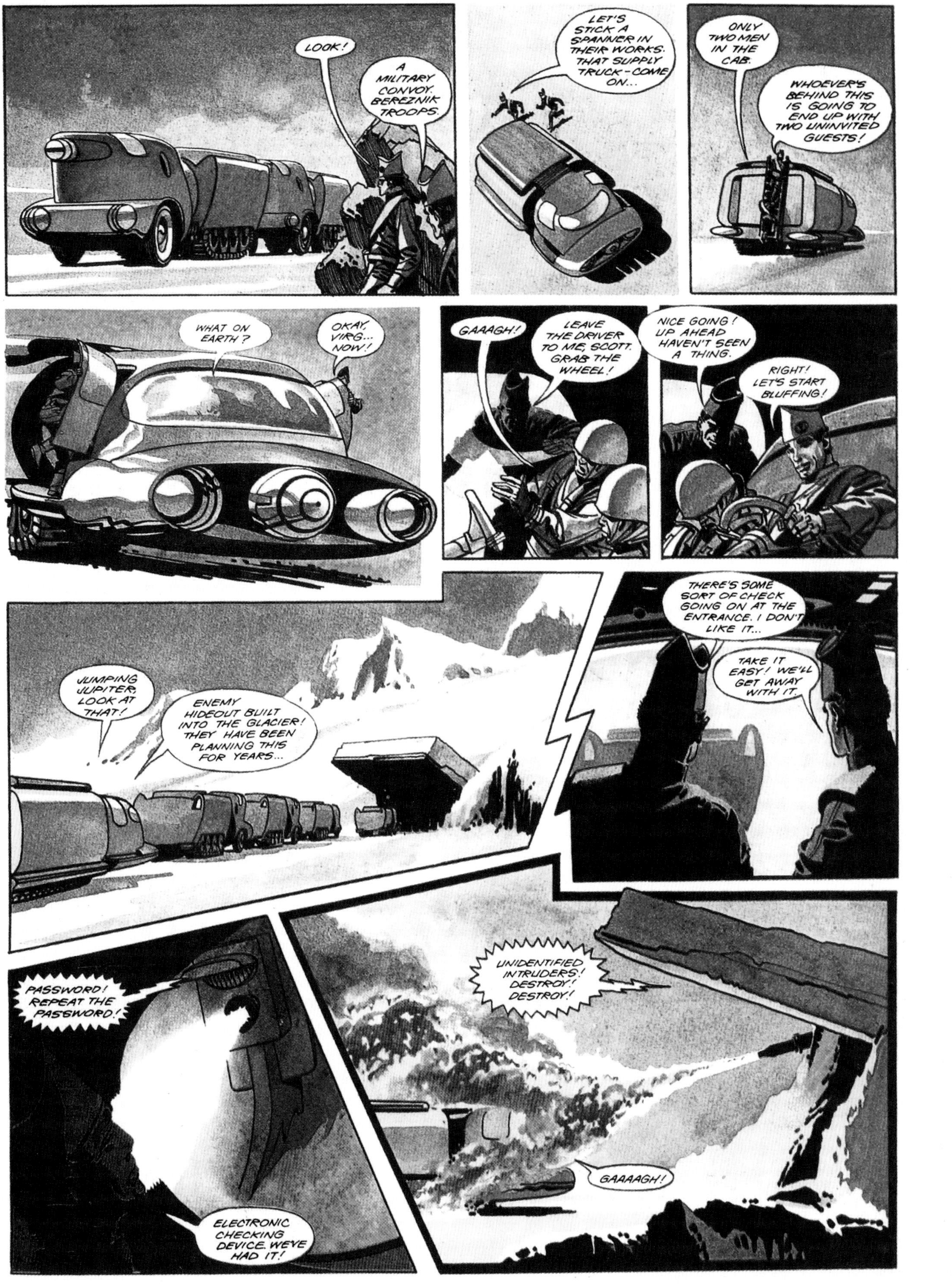
LOOK!
A MILITARY CONVOY. BEREZNIK TROOPS.
LET'S STICK A SPANNER IN THEIR WORKS. THAT SUPPLY TRUCK – COME ON...
ONLY TWO MEN IN THE CAB.
WHOEVER'S BEHIND THIS IS GOING TO END UP WITH TWO UNINVITED GUESTS!
WHAT ON EARTH?
OKAY, VIRG... NOW!
GAAAGH!
LEAVE THE DRIVER TO ME, SCOTT. GRAB THE WHEEL!
NICE GOING! UP AHEAD HAVEN'T SEEN A THING.
RIGHT! LET'S START BLUFFING!
JUMPING JUPITER, LOOK AT THAT!
ENEMY HIDEOUT BUILT INTO THE GLACIER! THEY HAVE BEEN PLANNING THIS FOR YEARS...
THERE'S SOME SORT OF CHECK GOING ON AT THE ENTRANCE. I DON'T LIKE IT...
TAKE IT EASY! WE'LL GET AWAY WITH IT.
PASSWORD! REPEAT THE PASSWORD!
ELECTRONIC CHECKING DEVICE. WE'VE HAD IT!
UNIDENTIFIED INTRUDERS! DESTROY! DESTROY!
GAAAAGH!

Part 5 - dateline 03 February 2068

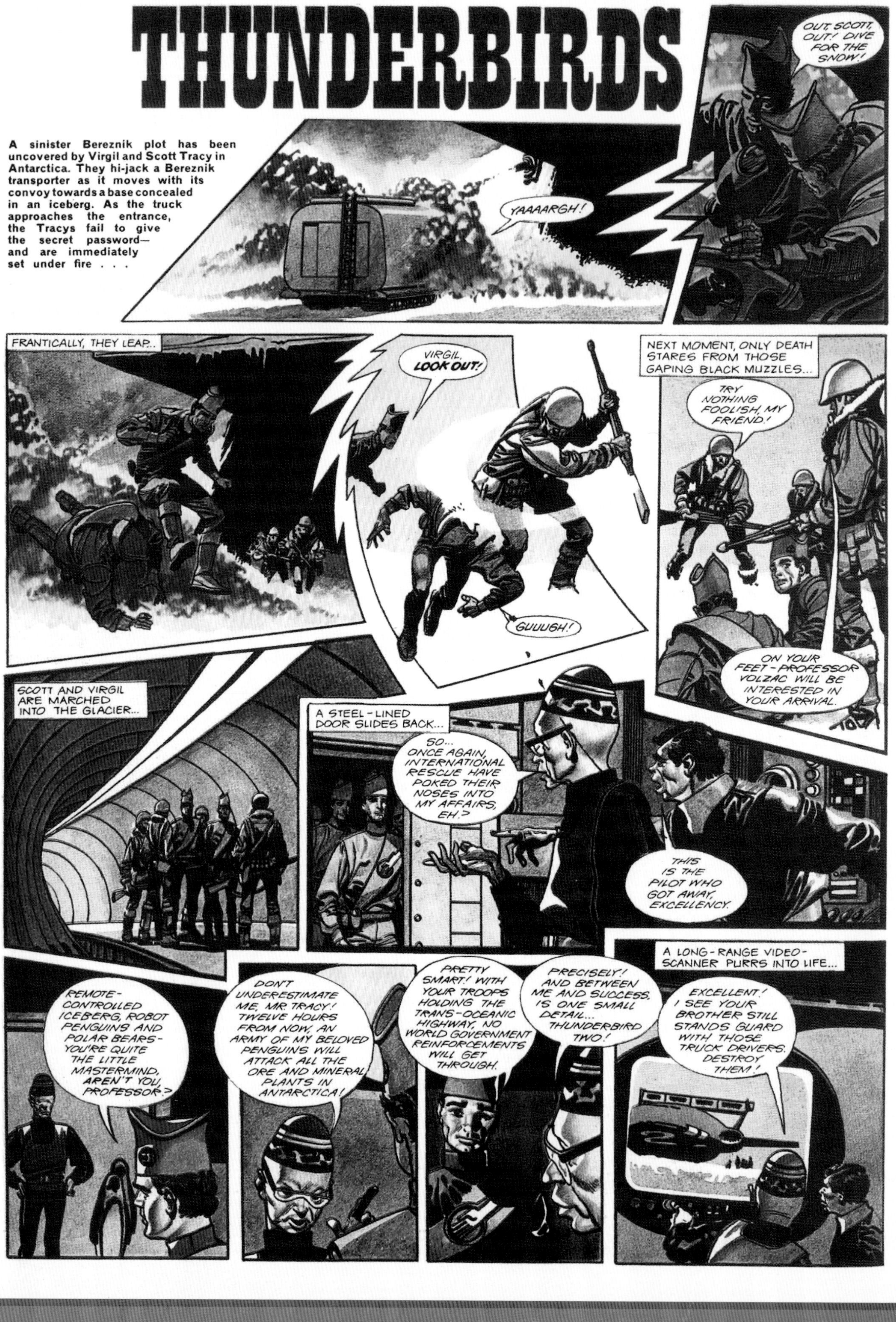
THUNDERBIRDS
A sinister Bereznik plot has been uncovered by Virgil and Scott Tracy in Antarctica. They hi-jack a Bereznik transporter as it moves with its convoy towards a base concealed in an iceberg. As the truck approaches the entrance, the Tracys fail to give the secret password— and are immediately set under fire . . .
YAAAARGH!
OUT, SCOTT, OUT! DIVE FOR THE SNOW!
FRANTICALLY, THEY LEAP...
VIRGIL, LOOK OUT!
GUUUGH!
NEXT MOMENT, ONLY DEATH STARES FROM THOSE GAPING BLACK MUZZLES...
TRY NOTHING FOOLISH, MY FRIEND!
ON YOUR FEET - PROFESSOR VOLZAC WILL BE INTERESTED IN YOUR ARRIVAL.
SCOTT AND VIRGIL ARE MARCHED INTO THE GLACIER...
A STEEL-LINED DOOR SLIDES BACK...
SO... ONCE AGAIN, INTERNATIONAL RESCUE HAVE POKED THEIR NOSES INTO MY AFFAIRS, EH?
THIS IS THE PILOT WHO GOT AWAY, EXCELLENCY.
REMOTE-CONTROLLED ICEBERG, ROBOT PENGUINS AND POLAR BEARS- YOU'RE QUITE THE LITTLE MASTERMIND, AREN'T YOU, PROFESSOR?
DON'T UNDERESTIMATE ME, MR TRACY! TWELVE HOURS FROM NOW, AN ARMY OF MY BELOVED PENGUINS WILL ATTACK ALL THE ORE AND MINERAL PLANTS IN ANTARCTICA!
PRETTY SMART! WITH YOUR TROOPS HOLDING THE TRANS-OCEANIC HIGHWAY, NO WORLD GOVERNMENT REINFORCEMENTS WILL GET THROUGH.
PRECISELY! AND BETWEEN ME AND SUCCESS IS ONE SMALL DETAIL... THUNDERBIRD TWO!
A LONG-RANGE VIDEO-SCANNER PURRS INTO LIFE...
EXCELLENT! I SEE YOUR BROTHER STILL STANDS GUARD WITH THOSE TRUCK DRIVERS. DESTROY THEM!

Artist: Frank Bellamy

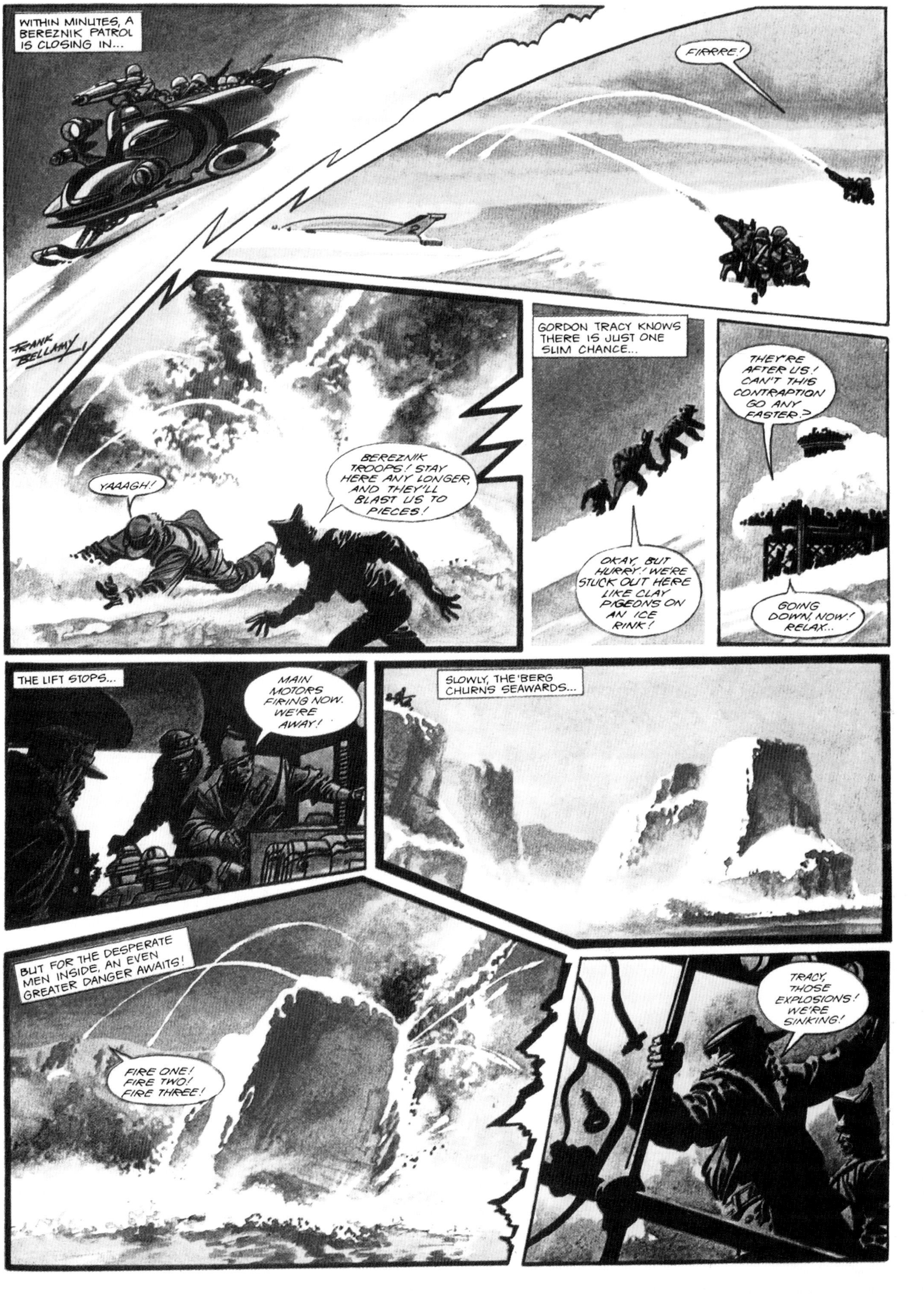
WITHIN MINUTES, A BEREZNIK PATROL IS CLOSING IN...
FIRRRE!
FRANK BELLAMY
YAAAGH!
BEREZNIK TROOPS! STAY HERE ANY LONGER, AND THEY'LL BLAST US TO PIECES!
GORDON TRACY KNOWS THERE IS JUST ONE SLIM CHANCE...
OKAY, BUT HURRY! WE'RE STUCK OUT HERE LIKE CLAY PIGEONS ON AN ICE RINK!
THEY'RE AFTER US! CAN'T THIS CONTRAPTION GO ANY FASTER?
GOING DOWN, NOW! RELAX...
THE LIFT STOPS...
MAIN MOTORS FIRING NOW. WE'RE AWAY!
SLOWLY, THE 'BERG CHURNS SEAWARDS...
BUT FOR THE DESPERATE MEN INSIDE, AN EVEN GREATER DANGER AWAITS!
FIRE ONE! FIRE TWO! FIRE THREE!
TRACY, THOSE EXPLOSIONS! WE'RE SINKING!

Part 6 - dateline 10 February 2068

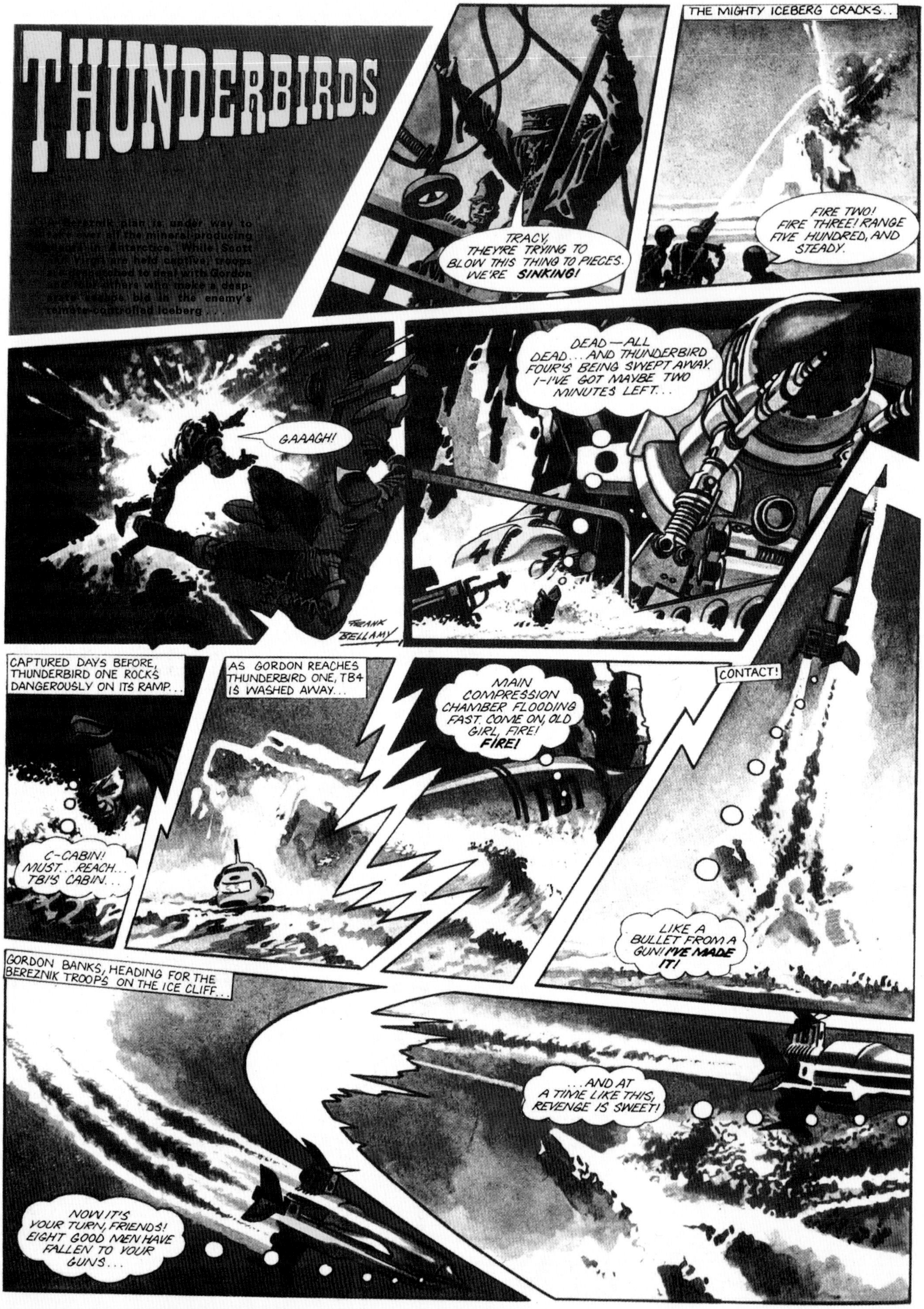
THUNDERBIRDS
plan is under way to
all the mineral-producing
in Antarctica. While Scott
Virgil are held captive, troops
to deal with Gordon
who make a desp-
escape bid in the enemy's
remote-controlled iceberg . . .
TRACY, THEY'RE TRYING TO BLOW THIS THING TO PIECES. WE'RE SINKING!
THE MIGHTY ICEBERG CRACKS...
FIRE TWO! FIRE THREE! RANGE FIVE HUNDRED, AND STEADY.
GAAAGH!
DEAD—ALL DEAD... AND THUNDERBIRD FOUR'S BEING SWEPT AWAY. I-I'VE GOT MAYBE TWO MINUTES LEFT...
FRANK BELLAMY
CAPTURED DAYS BEFORE, THUNDERBIRD ONE ROCKS DANGEROUSLY ON ITS RAMP...
C-CABIN! MUST... REACH... TB1'S CABIN...
AS GORDON REACHES THUNDERBIRD ONE, TB4 IS WASHED AWAY...
MAIN COMPRESSION CHAMBER FLOODING FAST. COME ON, OLD GIRL, FIRE! FIRE!
TB1
CONTACT!
LIKE A BULLET FROM A GUN! I'VE MADE IT!
GORDON BANKS, HEADING FOR THE BEREZNIK TROOPS ON THE ICE CLIFF...
...AND AT A TIME LIKE THIS, REVENGE IS SWEET!
NOW IT'S YOUR TURN, FRIENDS! EIGHT GOOD MEN HAVE FALLEN TO YOUR GUNS...

Artist: Frank Bellamy

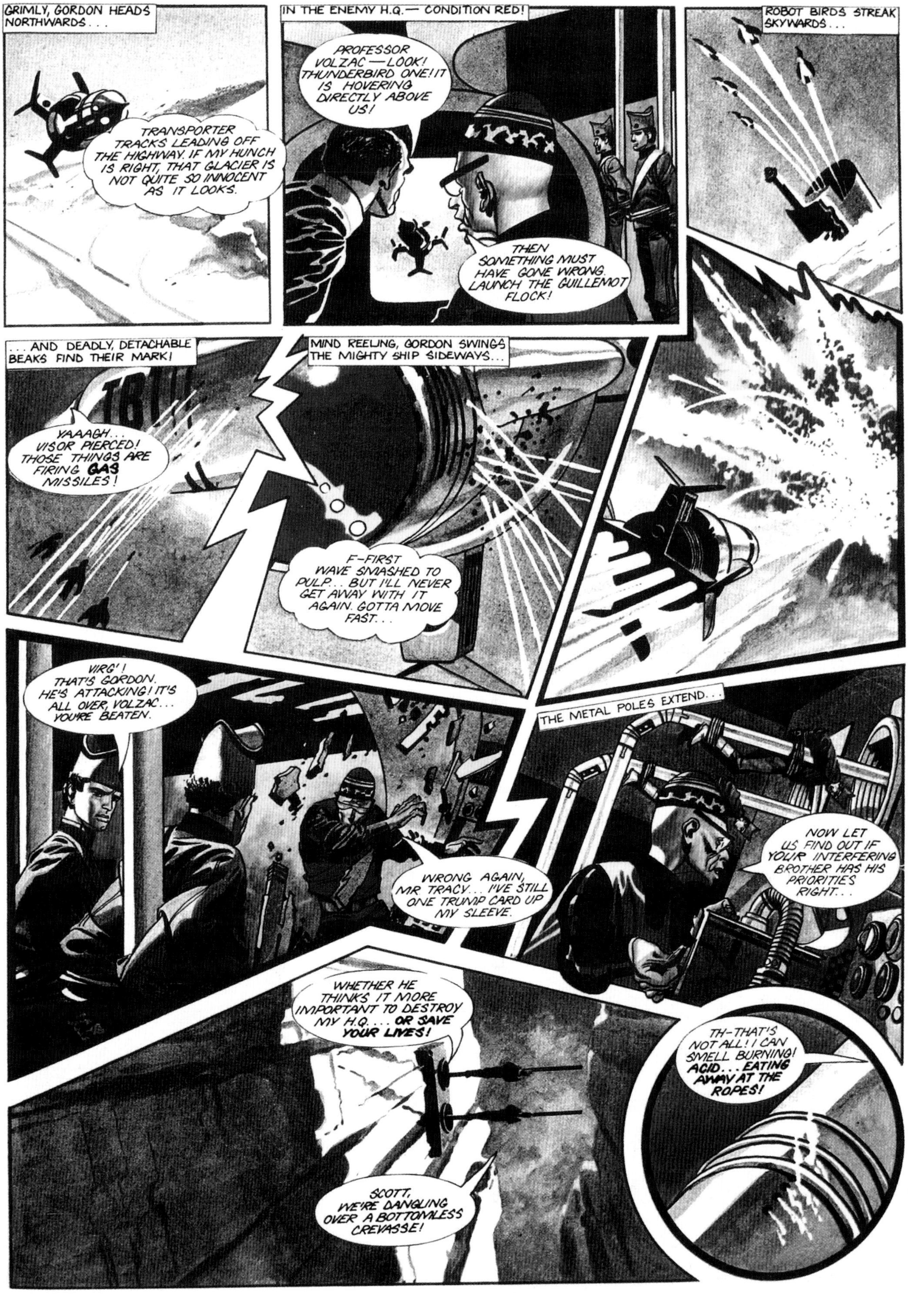
GRIMLY, GORDON HEADS NORTHWARDS . . .
TRANSPORTER TRACKS LEADING OFF THE HIGHWAY. IF MY HUNCH IS RIGHT, THAT GLACIER IS NOT QUITE SO INNOCENT AS IT LOOKS.
IN THE ENEMY H.Q. — CONDITION RED!
PROFESSOR VOLZAC — LOOK! THUNDERBIRD ONE! IT IS HOVERING DIRECTLY ABOVE US!
THEN SOMETHING MUST HAVE GONE WRONG. LAUNCH THE GUILLEMOT FLOCK!
ROBOT BIRDS STREAK SKYWARDS . . .
. . . AND DEADLY, DETACHABLE BEAKS FIND THEIR MARK!
YAAAGH... VISOR PIERCED! THOSE THINGS ARE FIRING GAS MISSILES!
MIND REELING, GORDON SWINGS THE MIGHTY SHIP SIDEWAYS . . .
F-FIRST WAVE SMASHED TO PULP... BUT I'LL NEVER GET AWAY WITH IT AGAIN. GOTTA MOVE FAST...
VIRG'! THAT'S GORDON. HE'S ATTACKING! IT'S ALL OVER, VOLZAC... YOU'RE BEATEN.
WRONG AGAIN, MR TRACY... I'VE STILL ONE TRUMP CARD UP MY SLEEVE.
THE METAL POLES EXTEND . . .
NOW LET US FIND OUT IF YOUR INTERFERING BROTHER HAS HIS PRIORITIES RIGHT...
WHETHER HE THINKS IT MORE IMPORTANT TO DESTROY MY H.Q.... OR SAVE YOUR LIVES!
SCOTT, WE'RE DANGLING OVER A BOTTOMLESS CREVASSE!
TH-THAT'S NOT ALL! I CAN SMELL BURNING! ACID... EATING AWAY AT THE ROPES!

Part 7 - dateline 17 February 2068

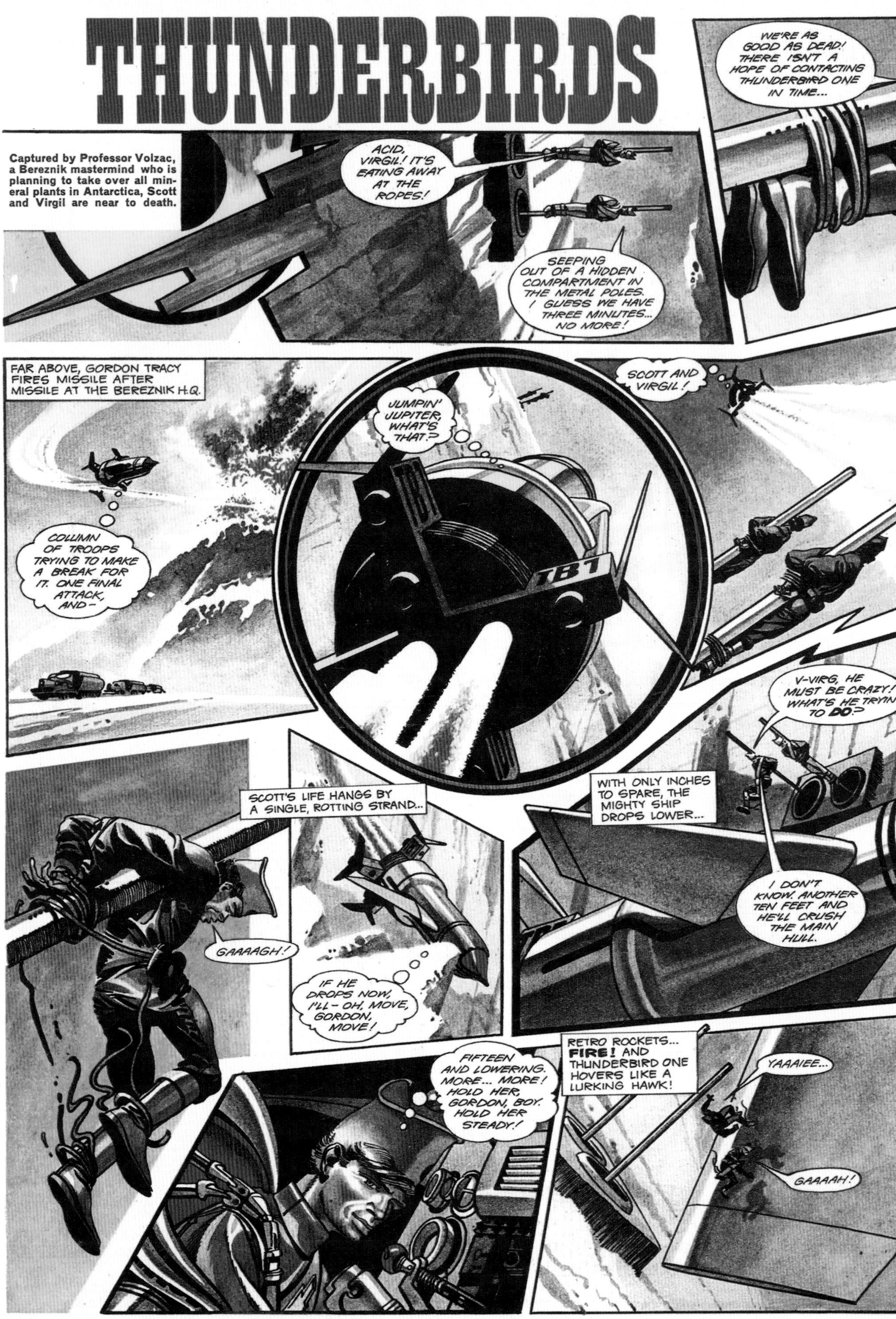
THUNDERBIRDS
Captured by Professor Volzac, a Bereznik mastermind who is planning to take over all mineral plants in Antarctica, Scott and Virgil are near to death.
ACID, VIRGIL! IT'S EATING AWAY AT THE ROPES!
SEEPING OUT OF A HIDDEN COMPARTMENT IN THE METAL POLES. I GUESS WE HAVE THREE MINUTES... NO MORE!
WE'RE AS GOOD AS DEAD! THERE ISN'T A HOPE OF CONTACTING THUNDERBIRD ONE IN TIME...
FAR ABOVE, GORDON TRACY FIRES MISSILE AFTER MISSILE AT THE BEREZNIK H.Q.
COLUMN OF TROOPS TRYING TO MAKE A BREAK FOR IT. ONE FINAL ATTACK, AND --
JUMPIN' JUPITER, WHAT'S THAT?
TB1
SCOTT AND VIRGIL!
V-VIRG, HE MUST BE CRAZY! WHAT'S HE TRYIN' TO DO?
SCOTT'S LIFE HANGS BY A SINGLE, ROTTING STRAND...
GAAAAGH!
IF HE DROPS NOW, I'LL - OH, MOVE, GORDON, MOVE!
WITH ONLY INCHES TO SPARE, THE MIGHTY SHIP DROPS LOWER...
I DON'T KNOW! ANOTHER TEN FEET AND HE'LL CRUSH THE MAIN HULL.
FIFTEEN AND LOWERING. MORE... MORE! HOLD HER, GORDON, BOY. HOLD HER STEADY!
RETRO ROCKETS... FIRE! AND THUNDERBIRD ONE HOVERS LIKE A LURKING HAWK!
YAAAIEE...
GAAAAH!

Artist: Frank Bellamy

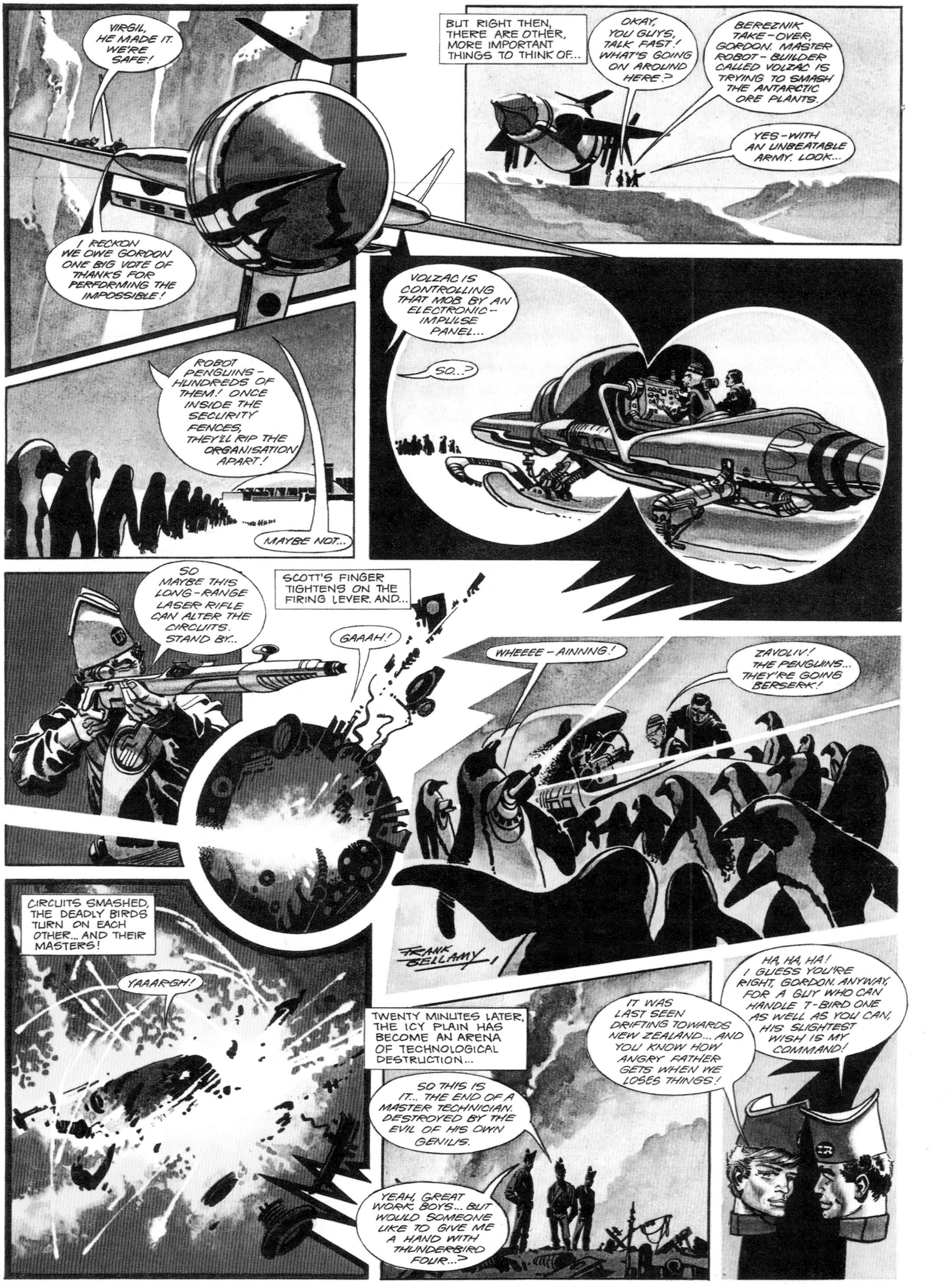
VIRGIL, HE MADE IT. WE'RE SAFE!
I RECKON WE OWE GORDON ONE BIG VOTE OF THANKS FOR PERFORMING THE IMPOSSIBLE!
BUT RIGHT THEN, THERE ARE OTHER, MORE IMPORTANT THINGS TO THINK OF...
OKAY, YOU GUYS, TALK FAST! WHAT'S GOING ON AROUND HERE?
BEREZNIK TAKE-OVER, GORDON. MASTER ROBOT-BUILDER CALLED VOLZAC IS TRYING TO SMASH THE ANTARCTIC ORE PLANTS.
YES-WITH AN UNBEATABLE ARMY. LOOK...
ROBOT PENGUINS - HUNDREDS OF THEM! ONCE INSIDE THE SECURITY FENCES, THEY'LL RIP THE ORGANISATION APART!
MAYBE NOT...
VOLZAC IS CONTROLLING THAT MOB BY AN ELECTRONIC-IMPULSE PANEL...
SO..?
SO MAYBE THIS LONG-RANGE LASER RIFLE CAN ALTER THE CIRCUITS. STAND BY...
SCOTT'S FINGER TIGHTENS ON THE FIRING LEVER. AND...
GAAAH!
WHEEEE - AINNNG!
ZAVOLIV! THE PENGUINS... THEY'RE GOING BERSERK!
FRANK BELLAMY
CIRCUITS SMASHED, THE DEADLY BIRDS TURN ON EACH OTHER... AND THEIR MASTERS!
YAAARGH!
TWENTY MINUTES LATER, THE ICY PLAIN HAS BECOME AN ARENA OF TECHNOLOGICAL DESTRUCTION...
SO THIS IS IT... THE END OF A MASTER TECHNICIAN. DESTROYED BY THE EVIL OF HIS OWN GENIUS.
YEAH, GREAT WORK, BOYS... BUT WOULD SOMEONE LIKE TO GIVE ME A HAND WITH THUNDERBIRD FOUR..?
IT WAS LAST SEEN DRIFTING TOWARDS NEW ZEALAND... AND YOU KNOW HOW ANGRY FATHER GETS WHEN WE LOSES THINGS!
HA, HA, HA! I GUESS YOU'RE RIGHT, GORDON. ANYWAY, FOR A GUY WHO CAN HANDLE T-BIRD ONE AS WELL AS YOU CAN, HIS SLIGHTEST WISH IS MY COMMAND!

TB1
TB1

CLASSIC COMICS

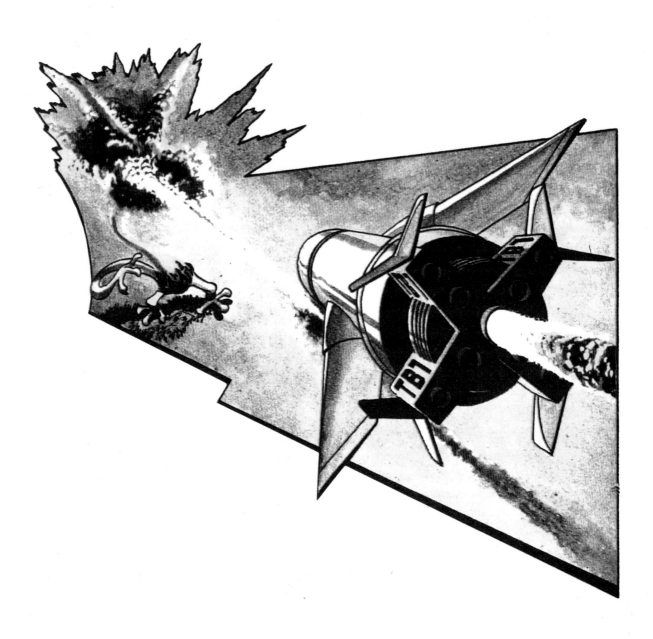

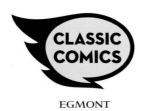

EGMONT